MEAT FOR MEN

LEONARD RAVENHILL was born in 1907 in the city of Leeds, in Yorkshire, England. After his conversion to Christ, he was trained for the ministry at Cliff College. It soon became evident that evangelism was his forté and he engaged in it with both vigor and power. Eventually he became one of England's foremost outdoor evangelists. His meetings in the war years drew traffic-jamming crowds in Britain, and great numbers of his converts not only followed the Saviour into the Kingdom, but into the Christian ministry and the world's mission fields. In 1939, he married an Irish nurse, and from that union have come three sons. Paul and David are themselves ministers of the gospel, and Phillip is a teacher. Leonard and his wife now live near Lindale, Texas, from which place Ravenhill travels to widely scattered preaching points in conference ministry.

MEAT FOR MEN

Leonard Ravenhill

Bethany Fellowship INC.
MINNEAPOLIS, MINNESOTA 55438

Meat for Men
Leonard Ravenhill

Thirteenth printing, 1980

Library of Congress Catalog Card Number A-510418

ISBN 0-87123-362-2

Copyright © 1961
Leonard Ravenhill
All Rights Reserved

Published by Bethany Fellowship, Inc.
5820 Auto Club Road, Minneapolis, Minnesota 55438

Printed in the United States of America

To

my sons

PAUL GRANDISON

DAVID MARTYN

PHILIP LEONARD

for whom

I covet

THE BURDEN OF THE LORD

Other books by Leonard Ravenhill

Sodom Had No Bible
Why Revival Tarries
America Is Too Young to Die
Revival Praying

CONTENTS

FOREWORD

It is indeed a pleasure to write a foreword to this challenging book. *Meat For Men* is exactly what the title implies; only those Christians who are *men*, or who want to be *men*, will approve of this diet. Mr. Ravenhill writes as he preaches. He holds no punches. He does not "beat the air." He makes every blow count. And *blow* it is—to sin, to carnality, and to easy living.

Mr. Ravenhill's call to prayer is strong because he prays. His challenge to discipline is impressive because he disciplines himself; he knows what self-denial and sacrifice mean. He calls to the highest—and the call finds a response in those who want, as he does, to hold the torch high.

I have had the privilege of both living with him and working with him. But the greatest is that of praying with him. He practices what he preaches. That is why he can be so hard on others and be loved for it, for what he imposes on others, he has first imposed on himself.

Twice he has been at death's door. (Once he had to jump from the fourth floor window of a burning hotel to the ice-crusted pavement below.) But it is not closeness to death that has made him what he is and caused him to write as he does. *That* he has learned in the prayer closet. He has heard God's heartbeat. This book is a call to others to come and hear it too.

When a young man at Cliff College, he was challenged by Principal Chadwick's prayer life. Not assured of his own ability to preach, Mr. Ravenhill committed himself to God as one who would pray. But God has made him a preacher and a writer too. Or did he become a preacher and writer because he prayed?

He has lived with men of prayer, both ancient and modern, and has found the same spirit that inspired them. He is incapable of reconciling the contradiction of a prayerless Christian. This latest book, *Meat For Men*, is an attempt not to reconcile but to solve this problem.

We unhesitatingly commend this book to all who are willing to be stirred, and who in turn will stir others. May God be pleased to use it to stir each of us—even as is so well expressed in Mrs. A. Head's hymn:

> Stir me, oh stir me, Lord, till prayer is pain,
> Till prayer is joy, till prayer turns into praise;
> Stir me, till heart and will and mind, yea all
> Is wholly Thine to use through all the days.
> Stir, till I learn to pray exceedingly;
> Stir, till I learn to wait expectantly.

T. A. Hegre
President
Bethany Fellowship

Recently we visited an elaborate and opulent temple in the Far East. This experience reminded me of one Christian visitor who, overwhelmed with the ornate place and its static wealth, asked a heathen worshipper, "What is the actual cost of erecting a temple like this?" The startled devotee replied in pained surprise, "What is the cost? This temple is for our god, and for him we never count the cost."

Such has also been the policy of Bethany Fellowship Missionary Training Center, where this book is printed. It is a school dedicated to training young men and women for the mission field. The staff, sanctified for the Master's use, have sought to make actual the words of the ancient prayer,

> Teach us, good Lord,
> To serve Thee more faithfully;
> To give and not to count the cost;
> To fight and not to heed the wounds;
> To toil and not to seek for rest;
> To labour and not to ask for any reward
> Save that of knowing that we do Thy will,
> O Lord, our God. Amen.

While I accept full responsibility for the text and message of this book, it is really a team job. The staff has a hand in its revision and in the correction of the proofs, the students in printing the book. This printing experience will be invaluable to them in other lands where they will minister.

The other day a minister for whom I was preaching told the congregation that he had read my former book, *Why Revival Tarries*, for the fourteenth time. *Meat For Men* is a kind of sequel to it. Already good news from readers of its first edition encourage us to send forth a second edition, with the earnest prayer that it may both stimulate faith to pray and also may prepare for the end-time revival so sorely needed in this day of bankrupt human philosophies. God worketh for him that waiteth for Him.

Leonard Ravenhill

CHAPTER ONE

ASHAMED AT HIS APPEARING?

BEFORE the Church arises to shake the world, some obscure truth of God arises to shake the Church.

God's men spake (and still do speak) as they were "moved by the Holy Ghost." In the sixteenth century the stubborn monk, Martin Luther, trembled at the truth of justification by faith in the Lord Jesus Christ; *then*, he made the papacy tremble. Two centuries later, after the famous Aldersgate Street experience—which heaven, earth, and hell recorded at "about a quarter to nine on the 24th of May, 1738"—John Wesley, the Oxford don, was revolutionized by an operation of the Holy Spirit; *then* he went out to shake England loose from her paganism. Even so, this year needs to see some majestic challenge come to the Church that she might move in great revival power to save a tottering civilization—or what there is left of it that is worthy of redeeming.

None but a bigot or a blind man (which could be the same) would deny that the moving of the Spirit

13

at Azusa Street almost fifty years ago saw a new page written in church history. Ten thousand churches worldwide testify to this fact (though from within and without, today's testimony is that that church, too, has lost much of its momentum).

It pleases the Lord to let the writer get scores of invitations from almost all branches of the fundamental churches in this and other countries. Everywhere the cry of pastors is something like this: "I trust the Lord will bring you this way. I have a large church. We have no financial problems, but oh, there is no brooding of the Holy Spirit over us." Then there is the added (and with justification, I say) terrible confession, "Our young people have never seen revival." Certainly no one man, no hundred men (though each lives to be as old as Methuselah) could hope to make even a surface scratch on the need of these churches.

Is there then a forgotten truth from the holy and imperishable Word of the living God that could shake this Laodicean Church from its creeping paralysis? I believe there is. If there is no word from the Lord in this hour, there certainly is no word for the Church from anyone else. One day I grasped two handfuls of books of sermons and found that not one of them had a message on the judgment seat of Christ.* This, I am persuaded after much thought, is the most neglected part of eschatology. Sermons there are and

*A book dealing solely with the judgment seat of Christ will soon be published by this author.

books without number on the Second Coming of Christ, but books dealing as a sole subject with the judgment seat of Christ can be counted on one hand. Why is this? Does meditation on such a penetrating truth terrify the minister? Well it might!

Unsupported by friend, wife, or attorney, each one of us must one day stand before Jehovah's *awful* throne. Each saint or sinner will be the cynosure of billions of eyes. The blazing eyes of the King of kings will pierce each one, and an impeccable record will interpret the life of each of us. Since there are no tears in heaven, it must be that at this fearful judgment seat "God shall wipe away all tears from their eyes." With time and human life behind us and beyond recovery, without possible means of correction, one thinks of the lines of Omar Khayyam:

> "Nor all your piety nor all your wit
> Can lure it back to cancel half a line—
> Nor all your tears wash out a word of it."

I cannot think of John Wesley, or Stephen Grellet, or many of the old soul-winners and prayer-warriors being ashamed at His appearing, but I am not so sure about myself on that day. How about you?

According to the Apostle Peter there are Scriptures "hard to be understood," not, I think, because they are irrational or morally unacceptable, but because they are intricate or considered a not-too-important part of a pattern. On the other hand, it *could be* that some Scriptures lie neglected for *this* offence: they reveal

the severity of God which is distasteful to the flabby
"believeism" of this hour. Judgment comes under this
classification of rejected or neglected truth. If the mod-
ernists reiterate that the love of God cannot be over-
stated, they need to be reminded that the justice of God
cannot be understated. The fact that *all* men are judg-
ment-bound is the most sobering thought I know.

With the slick phraseology of modern salesmanship,
the masses are being gulled into buying a sun tan lo-
tion—applied just from a bottle—that gives the color
without the user's ever seeing the sun! It seems to me
we are advertising and advocating a Christianity that
has the color but not the character of the real thing.
Anything in the spiritual life that savors of discipline
or of really "taking up the cross" is termed legalism
and is despised; on the other hand, what some call
liberty is but self-granted license.

With what reverence we stoop to enter the cell of
some old anchorite or mystic. At times each of us has
refreshed his jaded spirit by dropping his bucket into
the well of the inspired life of some mystic. But without discipline these spiritual hermits or flagellants
would never have been heard of. Today, things are
different. To our condemnation we confess that this
rush age is molding our living, whereas *we* should
mold the age. In the palliating preaching of this hour,
for every one reminder that we are soldiers, we are
told ten thousand times that we are sons. But *can* we
have soldiers without having discipline?

There is today a pale, pathetic, and unflinching interpretation of the blessed gospel, which guarantees salvation as "a financially and socially upgrading experience"; then it finalizes the offer by "a superlative bonus in eternity and comfort world without end." How different was Paul's concept of a disciple of Christ! Look at his vivid interpretation: "I think God has exhibited us apostles as *the lowest of the low*—like gallows birds; for we have become a spectacle to the universe, both angels and men. We are fools for Christ's sake, while you are most prudent Christians; we are feeble while you are strong; we are in disgrace while you are honored. To this very moment we are starving, thirsty, ragged, battered tramps; we are like the dregs and scum of society" (C. H. Dobb's translation of I Cor. 4:19–23). What an angry outburst this is at the Christianity of Paul's day (and the Christianity of our day too), with vain effort to be acceptable to a Christ-hating world!

Again, learn a lesson from Moses. In the shattering experience of being tossed onto the backside of the desert for what must have seemed the interminable experience of forty years—and after almost forty years of the lordly life of a prince in Egypt—Moses was saved by two immutable experiences: one, he "endured as seeing him who is invisible"; the other, his concept of the judgment day—namely, "he had respect unto the recompence of the reward."

Beloved, this is the hour for us to "labor to be accepted of him." Unused and therefore unproductive hours are stacked up against us to be accounted for in that great day when the books shall be opened. At this hour our Saviour, the Christ of God, is seated on the throne of mercy. Frederick William Faber speaks of it this way:

> "My God, how wonderful Thou art!
> Thy majesty how bright!
> How beautiful Thy mercy seat,
> In depths of burning light!"

However, one also thinks of the judgment seat not as beautiful but, in the language of Isaac Watts, as "Jehovah's awful throne." My earnest prayer is that from this simple study of a profound eternal truth, we may so "step up" our spiritual living that what we are (and from what we *are* flow all actions, attitudes, etc.) will abide in the day of Christ's coming, so that we shall not be ashamed at His glorious appearing.

CHAPTER TWO

THE UPPER-ROOM MEN

G OD-HUNGRY men find God. As the hart pant-
eth after the water brooks, so the souls of the
Upper-Room crowd panted for the living God. Spiritually naked, they fled to Him that they might be
clothed upon with the blessed Spirit. Empty, they
craved to be filled. Powerless, they tarried until they
were endued. Bankrupt and beggar-like, they pled the
riches of His grace. Then this *fear*-filled crowd became *fire*-filled messengers. Though swordless, these
soldiers of Christ fought the might of imperial Rome
and won. Though without ecclesiastical prestige, they
opposed the frozen orthodoxy of sterile Judaism and
pierced it to the heart. Unlettered, they unblushingly
declared the whole counsel of God and eventually
staggered the intellectual Greeks.

Without question, the greatest need of this hour
is that the Church shall meet her ascended Lord
again, and get an enduement that would usher in the
revival of revivals just before the night of nights settles
over this age of incomparable corruption.

My guess is that the waiting host in the Upper Room never anticipated the rushing, mighty wind, were staggered by the tongues of fire, and were all amazed that they had utterance they could not define. To say that these folk were all backsliders a-waiting another touch from God is to twist truth. Backsliders are the most joyless folk in the world, but these disciples, having seen the Master recently ascend to heaven in a cloud, had returned to Jerusalem with great joy. They had fled to the Upper Room to await the promise of the Father. That meant they were obedient; backsliders are disobedient. After Christ's ascension they worshipped Him; backsliders forsake Him. No, let's get this straight: these were a happy people, an obedient people, a worshipping people, a praying people.

Yes, this was *a praying Church*. In the Jordan while Jesus prayed, the Spirit descended upon Him; and in the Upper Room while the disciples prayed, the blessed Spirit descended upon them. Let's keep this to the forefront in our thinking: the Spirit comes upon praying people. That which He did in the past, that He will do again.

This was *a concerned Church*. In the Upper Room every known step they could take had been taken in obedience to the divine command. These inadequate men longed to be adequate so that the world might know He had sent them.

This was *a contrite Church*. In the Upper Room

these men were plagued with their own spiritual in-
fidelity. They had failed Him; some had lied about
Him; some had doubted Him; all had forsaken Him.
What a wailing wall that Upper Room must have
been! Was there ever such a Valley of Baca? Were
the angels ever so busy storing tears—bitter, scalding,
salty tears—into the bottle of memory as in those ten
days? These men were rending their hearts and
not their garments. Their harps were on the willows.
An old mystic once said, "There are only two places
for God's people—in the dust and in heaven." Only
in one or the other are we safe. These men in quest
of the Spirit were in the dust—blessed dust—better
than gold dust if in our prostration we seek the power
of the Lord and see His glory!

This was *a confessing Church*. In that Upper Room
no man ran his theological inch tape over his neigh-
bor. They were all *with one accord*. No lip shot out
in criticism; no finger pointed at a supposed leakage
that hindered the coming of the promised power. *All*
were self-admitted bankrupts. Here is a classic exam-
ple of God's people, called by His name, humbling
themselves and seeking His face; and God in turn hearing them and sending through an otherwise paralyzed
arm a wave of supernatural power. They waited on
the Lord and renewed their strength.

Today no one has time to wait. Some argue there
is no need to wait for the coming of the Spirit because He has already been given. I am sure they are
right. But I am equally sure there is need to wait so

that we can take a Spirit-conducted tour around our own hearts. We need to say with Croly:

> "Spirit of God, descend upon my heart,
> Wean it from earth, through all its pulses move;
> Stoop to my weakness, mighty as Thou art,
> And make me love Thee as I ought to love."

The common offer of evangelists these days is this: "You need power; come to the altar and get it." This has no more moral appeal than taking a car for gas and saying to the attendant, "Fill her up." This shibboleth brings no moral change or spiritual enduement that would make a sin-sick world and a flabby faltering Church know that the Almighty has visited His people. Obviously He has not.

In this evil hour of aggressive, atheistic philosophy and passive Christianity (so-called), we need a Mordecai with a broken heart but a resolute will to lead us all in sackcloth and ashes. God pity us that we have swung from the Upper Room with its fire to the church with the supper room and its smoke.

CHAPTER THREE

TODAY'S SLEEPING GIANT

SOLEMNLY and slowly, with his index finger extended, Napoleon Bonaparte outlined a great stretch of country on a map of the world. "There," he growled, "is a sleeping giant. Let him sleep. If he wakes, he will shake the world." That sleeping giant was China. Today, Bonaparte's prophecy of some one hundred and fifty years ago makes sense.

Transfer Napoleon's statement to the realm of the spiritual, and substitute Lucifer for the growler Napoleon, and the Church of Christ for China. Then you can almost see the fire belch from between Lucifer's teeth and almost behold the fear in his eyes as he thinks of the Church's unmeasured potential and growls, "Let the Church sleep! If she wakes, she will shake the world." Is not the Church the sleeping giant of today?

Some months ago the newspaper headlines carried the story of a young Chinese student who "flunked" his exams here in America. So humiliated was he and

so withered by anticipated scorn that for three years
the youth hid in the belfry of a church and became
skin and bones. Because of his shame, he froze in
winter and blistered in summer under that church's thin
roof. As today's Church of Jesus Christ thinks on the
day of reckoning that is surely coming, oh that a holy
fear would come upon her (even if it drives her to
extremes) in order to arouse her from her present
paralysis!

Consider Samson's fall. He didn't get drunk; he
didn't commit murder; he didn't steal. Samson fell
simply because he succumbed to the natural, and fell
asleep. That one small act put him into captivity,
made a false god popular, and scattered the forces of
the true and living God. Remember, Samson was not
the man with the bulging biceps and mountains of
muscle interpreted by medieval artists and Bible
painters. Nor was he taller than other men or broad-
er. But the challenging fact is that Samson was different from other men—manifestly different.

Samson's enemies knew that he was different from
others. Through Delilah, the woman of the world,
hear these enemy-leaders put a bribed question to
God's superman: "Tell me wherein thy great strength
lieth and wherewith thou mightest be bound to
afflict thee" (Judges 16:6). Delilah herself knew that
Samson was different. But most moving of all, Samson
himself knew he was different, for he said, "Bind me
with seven green withs. . . , then shall I be *weak and
be as another man*" (vs. 7). On another occasion he

admitted, "Bind me with new ropes . . . , then shall I be . . . *as another man*" (vs. 11); and later, "If I be shaven, then . . . shall I *become weak,* and *be like any other man*" (vs. 17).

If even yet you feel a hangover of the old interpretation that the Samson of the Bible is a distant relative of Hercules or Atlas (famed in mythology for carrying the world on his back), then think again. Samson was no human monstrosity. He was no superedition of a Goliath. If Samson had been a colossus, then why did Delilah ask the question, "Wherein lieth thy great strength?" Let the final word be from the Word of God itself, for in telling the story of men mighty in faith, the writer of the Hebrews terminates: "Time would fail me to tell of Gideon, of Barak, of Samson, . . . who *through faith* . . . stopped the mouths of lions." (Only two men in Scripture stopped the mouths of lions—Daniel and Samson.) But no giant could singlehandedly, as Samson, "put to flight the armies of the aliens," or toy with opposing armies. Here, Samson slays a thousand men with the jawbone of an ass; there, he kills another thirty men. Here, he takes the gates of Gaza for a ride; there, he tears a lion like paper; and to add insult to injury, the Spirit's comment is "he had nothing in his hand."

Note well, yea, read for yourself the whole story of the secret of this mighty exploiter, this more-than-conquering believer: *"The Spirit of the Lord rested mightily upon him."* Everything in the story adds up to this staggering fact: *Supernatural power was upon Samson.*

Now turn back ten chapters in this wonder book of Judges and have a little peep into the life of Gideon. Surely as a boy, Gideon had heard from his father the hair-raising stories of a mighty Deity. More than once, I am sure, he had sat on his grandpa's knee and heard of the window in heaven from which God had shared angels' food with Israel. Little Gideon thrilled as he was told of Israel's race to the Red Sea, with a mad Pharaoh pursuing; and then the magic of the waters parting to let the swordless armies through, while walls of water fell over the ironclad forces of Egypt. As the old grandfather told little Gideon the stirring story of the brazen serpent or else of the water that gushed from the rock, I, for one, can feel my own flesh "creep" with Gideon's.

In Judges 6 Gideon is older, and while threshing corn, is fearing an attack of the Midianites. For seven years, the once-liberated slaves of Pharaoh had again become captives. Dens and caves were their homes. No longer were they able to sing the Lord's song. It must have sounded like a fairy tale when that angel appeared to Gideon and informed him, "God is with thee, thou mighty man of valor." Yet he shot back the answer, "*If* God be with us, where be all his miracles which our fathers told us of?" This answer makes clear that Gideon was expecting some supernatural evidence. To him, the seal of the Lord's presence would be something that could not be rationalized.

Alas that today there is more evidence of religious sensation before our eyes than evidence of spiritual regeneration and supernatural phenomenon! Not many Christians today can forget the fact that the devil goeth about as a roaring lion, but we seem to have lost sight of the fact that the Lion of the tribe of Judah has defeated the roaring lion of hell, and that therefore every anointed Samson or Gideon or church can also slay the lion of hell. Though wicked men are doing wickedly (looking back just to 1949, who can forget this fact?), God's promise to us is that "the people that do know their God shall be strong and do exploits."

This much is sure: If we could merit revival by fasting, there would be many martyred by starving. If we could organize revival, we would pool our thinking to outwit the powers of darkness. If we could buy this elusive revival with the mammon of unrighteousness, we could get a score of what we call Christian millionaires (the term is a misnomer) to underwrite the thing for us. If we could blast the devil from this present world-dominion, we would pledge the politicians for an atom bomb. God pity us that after years of writing, using mountains of paper and rivers of ink exhausting flashy terminology about the biggest revival meetings in history, we are still faced with gross corruption in every nation, as well as with the most prayerless church-age since Pentecost.

Earlier in this chapter I made a plea for the return of the supernatural. Now for a word of explanation. For a decade, all over this land there has been a ministry of the miraculous (more or less), and thank God for all that honors Him and abides. But having said that, here is a plea for sane thinking and a spiritual evaluation of the evangelistic field. To a large degree have we not substituted seeing for hearing? In the Acts, Philip the evangelist could have transferred the Ethiopian eunuch to a city seething with revival fever where the eunuch could have seen "the lame leap like an hart and the tongue of the dumb sing." Instead, he pitched right into the Word of the living God, and beginning at the same Scripture preached unto him Jesus. Today we need Christ-centered teaching. Our crucified, exalted Christ must have pre-eminence over all other slants of truth, for while the Church is languishing, the world is perishing. "Arm of the Lord, awake and put on strength!"

Again let me say, Samson's size was not the secret of his strength. The fact that he was the same size after he backslid negatives the idea that he was a giant. His only external peculiarity was his long locks, uncut because he was a Nazarite. Nor had his long hair in itself any abnormal power. His hair meant shame—the putting forth of the finger, the shooting out of the lip, the caustic comment that Samson was like a woman.

Samson's secret was obedience. As long as Samson trod the straight and narrow path of obedience, he was invincible. J. H. Sammis was right when he wrote,

"Trust and obey, for there's no other way
To be happy in Jesus, but to trust and obey."

And obedience will be our strength too. Eyes will wonder, arguments will come to the mind, Lucifer will question why we should pray so much, sacrifice so much, and fast so often when the other fellow does not do it. Again the answer is "Whatsover he saith unto you, do it."

Samson's Nazarite vow also exempted him from wine and touching any dead thing—a simple argument for our separation from the world. Today, mixed teaching, mixed living, and mixed bathing "foul up" the Church of God.

Let us remember, too, that Samson, who began in the Spirit, fell into the flesh, and so had a prison term to bring him to his senses. Finally, by one last mighty miracle, he finished in the Spirit. Backslider, this is a word for your recovery, for God can restore the years that the cankerworm and the caterpillar have eaten. He who is able delights in mercy.

Samson's final act of power was the crowning achievement of a spectacular life's work. After he had slipped out from under the harness of obedience, he was forced into separation from the world in a prison. Once an army trembled at his very sight; later a single boy came to lead the blinded Samson into the temple of Dagon, the fish-god. How had the mighty fallen! Yet now, God took this "weak thing" into a temple full of lords of the Philistines and set him between the pillars. "Samson took hold of the pillars, the one with his right hand and the other with his left, and he bowed himself with all his might." Holy jealousy gripped him. Mighty as he had been in other things, Samson now proved mightiest in prayer: "Lord, strengthen me this once!" (Would to God that every professed believer in the whole of Christendom would borrow this prayer and mean it.) Then with dramatic conclusion, Samson sealed the doom of maybe ten thousand people—more in his dying than in his living, the Divine Record says.

Is this the dying hour of this dispensation? Many say it is. Some Christians have already hung their harps on the willows, and yet others seem to delight in speaking of the Church's present lapse as a proof of divine inspiration. But I myself believe that if the Church will only obey the conditions, she can have a revival any time she wants it. The problem of the Church is the problem in the garden of Gethsemane—sleep! For while men sleep, the enemy (false cults) sow their seed. Lest men sleep the sleep of eternal death, O arm of the Lord, O Church of the living God, awake!

CHAPTER FOUR

THE HARNESS OF DISCIPLINE

TO some, this word *discipline* will have a monastic
flavor, for it smells of the Middle Ages or throws
onto the screen of the mind a picture of an unwashed
hermit or a hollow-eyed anchorite. Be not deceived. Every smart "top brass" military expert has arrived there
because he wore the harness of discipline. Leonard
Bernstein in his music-talks holds his baton like a magic wand over mesmerized millions *because* of discipline. This brings to mind the words of the poet:

"The heights by great men reached and kept
Were not attained by sudden flight,
But they, *while their companions slept,*
Were toiling upward through the night!"

In a brilliant sermon called "Discipleship," G.
Campbell Morgan says, "Jesus Christ could speak
to the sorrow-burdened heart of humanity words so
full of mother-love and father-love as to make men
crowd and press round Him. On the other hand, He
could suddenly speak words that flashed and scorched
and burned until men drew back in astonishment."
Bracketed in the last group would be these two com-

mands: "Take my yoke upon you"; and "My disciple, take up your cross and follow me." Both of these words imply discipline.

If any man wants to write a best seller, let him attempt a book on *How to be a Saint in Six Easy Lessons*. Such a writer would be fishing with bait that this generation of believers wants; but I, for one, would not swallow it.

A century back, believers entering church membership were given two books: a Bible, and a book on church discipline. But what brave pastor these days dares give his new members the latter book? Do you wonder that a contemporary writer says, "We Protestants are the most undisciplined people in the world"?

When we sing in a sunlit church "Oh to be like Thee; Oh to be like Thee," we get weepy and feel an emotional lift. But permit this simple challenge: Do we really mean "Oh to be like Thee"—like the Christ of God, who was a man of discipline? Do we really mean "Oh to be like Thee"—fasting alone in the desert? Do we mean "Oh to be like Thee"—so that without our wilting under it, the world can say of us as of Him, "He hath a devil"? Do we mean "Oh to be like Thee"— to touch the depths of prayer that make us cry, "All Thy billows are gone over me"? Do we mean "Oh to be like Thee"—to become habituates of the fastnesses of the prayer chamber? Do we mean "Oh to be like Thee"—in a will like His, for He said, "I *always* do the will of my Father"? Is not that discipline?

The religious sentimentalist who sings "Just a closer walk with Thee" but walks close to the ungodly and sits with the blasphemers in the bleachers is not to be taken too seriously. Be very sure, friend, that this vile world is *not* "a friend to grace to help me on to God." We need to pray the Father to put some blood into this "water" that runs through our veins. Our Simon-like natures need the Upper-Room fire to clean us out and the discipline of the Spirit to shape us into soldiers.

Three hundred years ago the saintly Samuel Rutherford, a master indeed in the art of soul culture, declared that he could praise God for "the hammer, the file, and the furnace." All three came Rutherford's way. His finishing school in grace was the Bass Rock, where the damp stones shone like the walls of "the city which hath foundations whose builder and maker is God." Rutherford's secrets were worship and discipline.

Just think of this: Severe as is the Order of the Trappists, a Cistercian Order introduced into the U.S.A. in 1848, it needs to keep building monasteries to house men who want a disciplined life. And often it gets the best brains too!

Maturity (mental, physical, or spiritual) is not "attained by sudden flight." When Maria Callas stepped out of a plane in Chicago (she was already the young empress of European opera), the reception group expected to find an egocentric virago. "Instead," said a member of that party, "she was a shy, quiet, discerning woman, modest as a pilgrim." In the rehearsal, in order to encourage the chorus, she sang the "Casta Diva" full-voiced nine times. The final result? "Chicago was awed, floored, flabbergasted." Her ultimate triumph, despite a boil as large as a silver dollar on the back of her neck, was this: twenty-two curtain calls and a seventeen-minute standing, screaming ovation. Maestro Tullio Serafin uncovered this amazing woman's secret weapon—an upper register that could out-coloratura any coloratura in the business.

But Maria Callas had opposition of the worst kind—her own weight. She was a 250-pound powerhouse. Four months of discipline brought her to a streamlined 130-pound classical figure that looked as though it had been "peeled off a Grecian urn." From discipline of body she turned to discipline of voice. This girl had begged the opera masters of the day to hear her; they were soon kneeling to be heard by her. Once she sought contracts; soon others were screaming for her signature to their contracts. She could hold at arm's length even the mighty La Scala Opera House, the Vatican of its tribe. At her coronation performance, the Queen of England clamored for Maria; South America worshipped her; London went mad. America alone held out against her; then it too succumbed. I am not interested that she could wear Christian Dior's most exclusive dresses and make an audience gasp with her self-owned million dollars' worth of jewelry except from this point of view: Without discipline, this girl would have been "just another chorus girl."

It was Dr. Douglas Freeman, the first man in the United States who ever got President Eisenhower thinking seriously about a political career, who said, "The word that described Robert E. Lee was duty; the word that described George Washington was patience." The word, then, that in turn describes Dr. Freeman is *discipline*. Any man who packed seventeen hours every day into creative work and could compress four full-time careers into his sixty-seven years as he did—namely, editor, historian and biographer, educator, broadcaster and lecturer; any man who has Dr. Freeman's appetite for redeeming the time (he had a goad over his desk reading, "Time Alone is Irreplaceable; Waste it Not") is worthy of the honorary degrees that twenty-seven universities across the nation conferred upon him. By some pitiable pretenders, Maria Callas, Douglas Freeman, and others of their like will be labeled fanatics. No such thing! They learned at least one thing: life is a one-way street with no second attempt for flunkers.

Twenty-five years of discipline in a crow's nest of an office up behind his church in Chicago brought about a Dr. A. W. Tozer, who produced a book, *The Pursuit of God*. This in turn produced on the ocean of spiritual teaching waves that lap their way to the ends of the earth.

Finally, see this: Before me is a copy of a soul-stirring, spirit-challenging book, *John Sung*, by Leslie T. Lyall (C.I.M. production). Read it and weep. Dr. Sung had a dynamic transformation by regeneration, but it cost him a stretch in the mental hospital at White Plains, New York. He jibbed at this. But who wouldn't? Then came the word of the Lord: "If you can endure this trial patiently for one hundred and ninety-three days, you will have learned how to bear the cross and walk the Calvary Road of unswerving obedience." The net result of his discipline—self-chosen—was that, incredible though it seems, at the end of the hundred and ninety-three days, Sung had read the Bible through forty times! Also, he had a key to understanding every one of the 1,189 chapters of the Bible. His greatest day, Sung declared, was when he graduated from the school of the Spirit—a mental home (sublime, sanctified humor!).

Here's the last string to my fiddle. After I spoke at a session in the Bible School of Wales, dear Mrs. Rees Howells called me for a private talk. We stood on the veranda of her home overlooking beautiful Swansea Bay. I can see her finger upheld as she said, "Many talk of my husband's buying this place with a shilling (fourteen cents) in his pocket. What they forget is that he prayed twelve hours a day for eleven months to know the mind of God." Brethren, that's discipline!

Here end our illustrations of discipline. But what illustrations!

Today, immediately one gets out of step with a near-by Christian, he is considered a legalist or smeared "over-spiritual." (I should write that word in capitals—think of it that way.) In "*that great day*" no man will be ashamed he was dubbed over-spiritual, though many will weep, groan, and "suffer loss" because of lack of discipline.

Discipline, then, is a harness by which we enable the Spirit to get the best out of our frail humanity. The Apostle Paul was a disciplinarian like his Master:

He disciplined his *body*: "I keep my body under."
He disciplined himself to *loneliness*: "All men forsook me."
He disciplined himself to *scorn*: "We are fools for Christ's sake."
He disciplined himself to *poverty*: "We suffered need."
He disciplined himself to *rejection*: "We are despised."
He disciplined himself to *death*: "I die daily."
He disciplined himself to *suffering*: "Persecuted, but not forsaken."

May this be our prayer, "Oh Lord, I bow *my* neck to *Thy* yoke!"

CHAPTER FIVE

AWAKE, SLEEPY GENERATION!

SINCE the hour Adam first rose to his feet, man has not stood, as today, between such potential and such peril. Yet, to stab awake our sleepy generation to the peril of the hour, even a Gibbons (the eminent historian of the masterly work, *The Decline and Fall of the Roman Empire*) could not flick his pen with enough skill. Nor could a Shakespeare strain adjectives or metaphors too far to reveal emphatically the progressive moral deterioration of this generation. Our scientists, too, are shouting from the housetops that they want to hurl man's body into the heavens with speeds of a lightning's flash—and not one second slower would hurl his soul into hell.

Without question, America is the richest nation in the world. It is a mighty crucible into which refugees of almost all modern nations are poured. It has far more Bible schools than any other nation. In these Bible schools is dedicated man power. Here, too, is wealth to get this man power to the ends of the earth, and here is linguistic ability unmatched in the annals of time.

Even the gathering at Pentecost had not the potential, humanly speaking, that this vast nation has. Do you wonder, then, that from every angle, hell has America under cross fire? This mighty land is *cursed with blessings.* I fear that unless she awakens, repents, and puts on the whole armor of God, she will be *blessed with cursings.* Already other nations are in slavery to communism or Catholicism. Can America and Britain long remain free?

In the Church of this day there is a wide-open gap in the ministry of the prophets. The chair of the prophet of the Lord is vacant. Some man could well plan to make history by filling it. (If there are any candidates for this ministry, we shall be glad to hear of them.)

At this very moment the eyes of the world are upon a prophet, though not a God-endued prophet. The cynosure of the world's eye is the cruel, Christless Khrushchev. How we need a Mordecai to ignore this Khrushchev, who is drenched with self-importance and drunk with the plaudits of half the world's empty-bellied multitudes that see in him a Joseph with granaries to feed them!

Deep within my own spirit I am convinced that in our day, unless we are to have the war of wars that will usher us into the night of nights and the judgment of judgments, we *must* have the revival of revivals. Pale, pathetic, palliating preaching must go. The pulpit never needed voices more than it does at this hour.

Does God wink at cultivated iniquity? Is the adultery of sophisticated moderns more palatable to God than the gross adultery of the bush native? No! Unless our hearts bleed in prayer, millions will soon bleed in the senseless slaughter of the greatest war that man has ever known. Let us recite this over and over until it burns in the brain and echoes in the Spirit-fired prayer meeting.

For the fifth straight year England reports another great drop in the membership of the Methodist Church, that once flamed throughout the world. Sixty-five per cent of the people in America, it is believed, are signed up with some church; but only twelve per cent of the nation is in church Sunday morning and only two per cent Sunday night.

Is it less than blasphemy to sing songs on Sunday such as "All that thrills my soul is Jesus," but spend hours in the week at ball parks or before T.V., trying to "get a kick" out of life? Does it make for anything like sincerity to sing so plaintively, "Now rest my long divided heart," when we are deeply aware of a vacuum within that gapes wider than the Grand Canyon? Can the world take us seriously when we believers say that we have meat to eat that it knows not of, and yet so often it sees us feed on the trash and garbage from modern magazines?

Ambrose Fleming called the resurrection of Jesus Christ "the best attested fact in history." Yet at Easter time, vain effort is made to rationalize the stupendous event of the Resurrection in order to try to save face before pseudo-intellectualism, which boggles at the fact that the Lord of glory died and rose again, triumphant over death, over hell, and over the grave. Who, then, can dispute the following biting statements of Murdo MacDonald in his book, *The Vitality of Faith*:

"Ever since the Renaissance, men have been trying to water down the Christian creed. Give us a religion purged of everything that defies logic, a religion stripped of the supernatural and emptied of miracle, a religion that is smooth and palatable and rationally acceptable—this has been the popular cry"?

Surely liberal Protestantism has gone out of its way to oblige.

The doom of this decaying civilization is spelled out in our crowded divorce courts, our all-time high of alcoholics, and the number of illegitimate births. Not long ago in the Hollywood area the police caught some intellectuals having a party—a mixed group of men and women all in the nude. (Fancy having to be an intellectual to carry on like that! Unlettered savages do the same.) Since they had no clothes on, this group could not be charged with having drugs in their possession, so were merely charged with moral vagrancy. What is our nation coming to?

Moreover, a news item says a boy of eight years with an I.Q. of 135 murdered his mother. This was premeditated, but the judge actually let the boy off and said no charge would be brought against him.

Furthermore, a Gallup poll shows that these days most people accept lying as part of everyday business. So there you have it. Virtue is scorned. Truth lies fallen in the street!

Somewhere in the archives of the British Admiralty at Whitehall, London, they have the record of a fine piece of maritime strategy. Ships of five nations were anchored in a bay in the South Pacific. A fierce storm was gathering offshore. The British captain decided to run, not away from the storm but into it. Everything available was battened down. Out crashed the ship into the boiling seas—pitching, tossing, rolling, and shuddering. Indeed, she did everything but go down. A couple of days later, buffeted but not broken, she returned to the port to find the ships of the other nations piled up on the beach.

The storm of the ages is about to break. Let the Church (each church) call its crew to a new dedication. Remembering that Christ is at the helm, and with Christ's Cross as our ensign, let us run into the storm. After the storm, we, too, shall return—to see upon the shores of time the battered, piled, wrecked, hell-inspired ideologies of the hour.

CHAPTER SIX

DRAW NIGH TO GOD

THERE are several reasons why some people cannot be approached. First, they are the great and mighty of earth, princes and potentates, who are behind high walls and are guarded. Or they are guarded for other reasons than greatness. Lunatics and criminals, for instance, might well be put in a safe place. In the areas where most of us circulate, there are also those we cannot approach because of a something in their attitude and sometimes because of something in our attitude. Then, too, there are some who would be willing to let us in, but others keep both them and us apart. A secretary, for instance, might deprive us of an interview with a willing person, so that for a paltry excuse we do not meet. Lastly, there are people who are afraid of losing friends, and so they keep a tight hold lest others draw near.

But here is a startling and stirring fact: I can get as near to God as my soul desires. Men cannot keep me from Him unless I let them; the devil cannot keep me from Him, though he may fight every inch of the way

as I proceed in prayer. It may be painful and penetrating to know, but the fact is that I am as spiritual
as I want to be, for who, with a grain of spiritual sense,
would think of crediting or rather discrediting God with
the responsibility for the low spirituality of this hour?

Intimacy with "the great" usually means favors.
A common saying among the redeemed is this, "God
has no favorites." But I think the whole of revealed
Truth completely destroys that premise. Closeness to
God inevitably leads to affection, and affection for Him
to yet greater nearness. The God-intoxicated person
ever thrills to sing, "Draw me nearer, nearer, nearer,
blessed Lord."

Drawing nearer leads in turn to strength. Would
not a man whose business economy has faltered feel
a new surge of confidence if offered the financial support of a millionaire friend? For the Christian, this
comparison is not strained, because the resources of
the infinite God are at the believer's disposal. What
a majestic prospect! Unlimited spiritual wealth, and
other wealth, is accessible to the human believing
soul. Everyone knows that knowledge *can* be power.
To the Christian, knowledge of these facts just given
is strengthening.

Nearness presupposes a mutual confidence. In the
spiritual realm nearness means love, and love is based
on confidence. In its very nature, love draws towards
someone, and in so doing draws away from others.
Since humans are not omnipresent, they have to choose

their company. We must either draw nigh to men and so draw away from God, or draw nigh to God and away from men. The choice, though not easy, is always ours. To the prayer closet, there is no conscription, but there *is* a constraint, a constraint of love. We may as well "settle" this once and for all—there are no short cuts to the high peaks of spirituality, and no ski lifts. One does not need to be an anchorite to live on "heaven's tableland," but there must be a practiced withdrawing. Love is an isolationist. Love has a supreme lover.

To the modern mind this policy of self-denial is austere. It seems to smell of the damp, cold Bass Rock, where Samuel Rutherford was incarcerated. Reflect a moment. Was there a thing Rutherford wanted while he was there? What are creature comforts if God is absent? What are absent comforts if God is present? Charles Wesley had traveled far on the highway of spiritual living to be able to write, "*Thou*, O Christ art *all* I want." Can I truthfully say *that?*

CHAPTER SEVEN

MODERN PHILOSOPHY AND THINKING —
ITS FALLACY

THE reason history repeats itself is that human
nature is ever the same. Thus the one thing we
learn from history is that we don't learn from history! I am just old enough to remember with an effort
the 1920's—their sky glowing with the dawn of a
new world order. Strange, isn't it, that this phrase
about a new world order, shouted from the housetops
after both world wars, has suddenly been dropped?
More than that, as a child they guaranteed me a war-
free world, and one secular prophet of that day (shun-
ning religion—indeed he mocked it) talked about the
inevitability of progress, the adequacy of materialism,
and the sufficiency of man.

Such optimism as this swept into *politics*, so that
in the British Parliament, Lord Curzon said that the
long dark night of barbarism had passed. We were
led to believe that the millennium, man-made, was
just around the corner. Then about 1937 a lady of
international stature, the leader of a famous religious
group, dared to prophesy that for a hundred years

there would be no world war. But there *was* one in two years!

Somebody also ventured the theory that progress in any shape or form was all a matter of *education*. In another half century, so the tale ran, all men would write like Shakespeare, paint like Raphael, think like Einstein, and invent like Edison. Poverty would soon be a bad memory. The humanists would pull down the hills of wealth and fill in the valleys of poverty.

Science, those past optimists told me, was the new messiah. With their ductless glands, they got both me and the rest confused. "Human love," they said, "depended on the interstitial, growth upon the pituitary, intelligence upon the thyroid, charity and kindliness upon the suprarenals. I was bamboozled, for it was plain to see that I was a cosmic accident, a mere bagful of chemicals, held together by a skin." Strange, isn't it, that for almost half a century glandular extracts have been on the market, and yet no new race of Christlike men have appeared. Now, to my horror, I know that I live in a shrinking world and an expanding universe. I know that while science has spent billions of dollars perfecting death rays and putting the death certificate for millions in one single bomb, it has not yet learned to put human kindness into a pill, nor has it a shot that can end human bitterness and clean the heart of man.

The next disturbers of my peace were the *psychologists*. Some of these said that we were all the crea-

tures of our environment. Tough, then, on the child
of the slums. After reflection, however, I remembered
that some of the very best men whom I knew had
come from the worst environments. Out of this human
jungle, a guiding Hand had brought miracles. So I
forgot the view of those men who tried to interpret
the race as a bundle.

Just then I met men on stilts confidently talking
of Freud, Jung, psychiatry; of Shaw's Christ, and
Einstein's finite universe; of time and space and the
fourth dimension; of theosophy, hypnotism, repres-
sion of the memory, supernormal faculties, the sub-
conscious mind, and finally, crystal gazing. These were
all offered as ways of peace, as escapes from the burden and heat of the day; but, alas, they were as tune-
less as a cracked bell.

In my workshop in those days I heard of the fail-
ure of the churches, of hypocrisy, etc. But then I
remembered men who, having gone to savage tribes,
always refused to carry arms for their own defense.
And what of those who entered areas famed for the
jungle scourge? For a wageless job in the steaming
jungles, had not scores left fame and fortune to offer
men Christ? Then, too, I reflected on the brilliant
men with whom I had worked. For years they had
been treading the intellectual treadmill but garnering
only husks. While quite young, two of them committed
suicide. These men had creature comforts, well-
stocked brains, confident philosophies, but with all

their scorn of religion were crippled with immoral
living.

And so, once and for all I settled the issue: *Life
will work only one way—God's way.* I took my Bible
to my workshop and read it. Some sneered, others
enquired, a few commended. I found that Christ could
and did change my life. And He could change other
lives. Often I have been ashamed of the Church; sometimes I have been ashamed of those who profess
Christ's Name; but never have I been ashamed of
Christ. Christianity has been weighed in the balances
and found difficult but not wanting. In the main it
has been rejected. For my part, I'm tired of clever
men. *The simple gospel believed, works!*

CHAPTER EIGHT

"IT'S *ME*, OH LORD"
(Psalm 51)

THE Bible, which we believe is the inspired and infallible Word of God, contains seventy books. The reason we say seventy over against the orthodox view of sixty-six is that the Book of Psalms is actually five books. In these five books there are one hundred and fifty psalms. Eighteen of these bear the name of David; eight of the eighteen are autobiographical; seven of the eight are penitential; one of the seven—namely, the fifty-first—is the greatest of these penitential psalms.

The structure of Psalm 51 is fascinating. In verses one and two David uses three words for sin: transgression, iniquity, and sin. In the same verses he uses three words for cleansing: blot out, wash, and cleanse. He mentions the word *broken* three times (in verses 8 and 17). He mentions the word *spirit* three times (in verses 10, 11 and 12).

If Mary Queen of Scots had been stained by adultery and murder as was David, she would have said she was "above the law." If Charles the First of England had been guilty of the same things, he would have overthrown Bathsheba. If James the Second had stood so condemned, he would have abrogated the seventh commandment. Queen Elizabeth the First in the same circumstances would have suspended Nathan. But David, king of Israel, did none of these things. Though, as he finished Psalm 139, David said, "*Search* me, O God, and *know* my heart: *try* me, and know my thoughts; and *see* if there be any wicked way in me, and lead me in the way everlasting" (vs. 23, 24), here in Psalm 51 he does not bare his heart to God. Here he is saying to the same God, "*Hide thy face* from my sins and *blot out all* mine iniquities." The lash of conscience within him is worse than the sting of the scorpion's tail. Guilt weighs on his spirit like a mountain range. He wrote Psalm 139 with boldness; he writes Psalm 51 with brokenness. He wrote Psalm 23 plucking the strings of a harp; he writes Psalm 51 plucking the strings of his heart. Here David does not slant his confession to anyone else. Here he makes no allusion to Bathsheba in any shape or form. Psalm 51 is painfully personal: "Purify *me...*, and *I* shall be clean: wash *me*, ... and *I* shall be whiter than snow. Make *me* to hear joy and gladness."

The great need of the hour is the Holy Spirit's unveiling of the human heart both to believers and unbelievers. The Spirit of God is the Spirit of Truth, who convicts of error; the Spirit of Fire, who convicts of coldness; the Spirit of Love, who convicts of hatred; the Spirit of Freedom, who convicts of bondage; the

Spirit of God, who convicts of human depravity; the Holy Spirit who makes bare human sin. Sin is not just a defect but a disease; not a mistake but madness; not error but enmity; not infirmity but iniquity.

In Psalm 51 from verses one to nine David is confessing the sins he himself has committed; in verse ten he shows anxiety about the sin he inherited; in verse twelve he is praying the prayer of a backslider. This Psalm is not written with ink but with blood. It is not punctuated with periods but rather with sobs and groans: "How are the mighty fallen!" Later, with his murder-mark erased from his spirit and having been delivered from his depravity, I am sure David outsang the angels as he declared, "He brought me up also out of an horrible pit and out of the miry clay."

You may be reading this message in the doctor's office, or in the stateroom of a ship. Maybe like David you too are condemned by sin and confused with it and concerned about it. To tell you that there is a place of deliverance sounds altogether too optimistic or too generous. Well, friend, the gateway to mercy, forgiveness, and cleansing is through the word David uses in the first verse: *Have mercy upon me.* The Apostle Paul uses this word in Ephesians 2:4 when he says, "God... is rich in mercy." Wesley uses it in his grand hymn:

> "'Tis mercy all, immense and free;
> For, O my God, it found out me."

If you will hate your sin, confess your sin, forsake your sin, kneel humbly at the feet of Christ and ask for forgiveness and for cleansing from your sin through His blood, as well as for the power of the Holy Spirit in your life, you too may be more than conqueror through Him who loved you. Then with Wesley you can sing,

"My chains fell off, my heart was free;
I rose, went forth, and followed Thee."

CHAPTER NINE

REPENTANCE OBSOLETE?

LANGUAGE is strained when one attempts to describe the Gospel as recorded by John the Apostle. Let me borrow some crutches here and use other men's opinions. Herder, the crusading theologian of the eighteenth century, said, "It seems that John's Gospel was written by the hand of an angel." Old Master Culness gets at it this way: "I believe that the writings of John have been blotted out by more penitents' tears and have won more hearts for the Redeemer than all the rest put together." Let Dr. A. T. Pierson complete this triad: "Matthew corresponds to the court of Israel, Mark to the court of the priests, Luke to the court of the Gentiles. John leads us past the veil into the holy of holies. Here is the inmost temple filled with the glory of God."

New interest in this Gospel of John was aroused in me in this way: I had preached at a certain conference, and the opinion was that there had been a real blessing. (This was gathered from the many expressions of the people.) Then came a letter. It read like this, "Dear

Mr. Ravenhill, I heard you preach two nights and was very disappointed because you stressed repentance." The writer added, "You should know that John's Gospel was the last one written and that John never uses the word repentance once. This proves that there is no need of repentance."

That argument is as useless as a swimming suit for a duck. If this letter writer knew that John wrote the last Gospel, he should have been well enough informed to know that John was also the human penman of The Revelation. That was John's last message, and in it he uses the word repent seven times. Repentance surely must have come back into fashion again!

Let us suppose that the writer of this letter is right. Using what is called the argument of silence, he says, "Because repentance is not in the Gospel of John, it is not legitimate to use it." Let us follow his argument for a few moments.

The word faith is used some 340 times in the New Testament, but *never once* is it used in John's Gospel. So faith goes out of the window? I can't preach on faith any more?

I am sure in my own mind that the brother who pilloried me for preaching repentance believes in hell. But does he know that not one of the terms used for hell (Gehenna, Tartarus, Hades) is ever used by John in his Gospel? So hell-fire preaching is out?

John's Gospel has no demoniacs, is silent about
lepers, seems never to have heard about children, omits
all mention of scribes, ignores the publicans, lists no
"Twelve," has not a parable in the whole Gospel, gives
no hint of a sect called the Sadducees, and does not seem
to have ever heard of the Sermon on the Mount. So I
cannot preach on these either?

On John's own confession, he is writing "that ye
might believe that Jesus is the Christ, the Son of God."
He uses the words believe or believed seventy-eight
times in his Gospel. But note: What we would think
essential to convincing people of the deity of Jesus, John
leaves out. He says, "The Word was made flesh," but
he does not even mention the virgin birth! Shall I stop
preaching this too?

John has no mention of the temptation of Christ,
nor of His transfiguration, nor of His ascension. He
makes nothing of the Lord's baptism, and totally fails
to mention the Gethsemane agony. The ministry of the
Son of God lasted more than one thousand days. John
records only about twenty of them. Am I out of order
to preach on the unmentioned 980 days? Dr. Edersheim,
writing the life of Christ without direct inspiration,
takes up no less than 1,524 pages, but John under direct
inspiration, in the Revised Version takes only thirty!
Is John to be charged with error because of omis-
sions? There are a dozen vital things mentioned by the
other Gospels that John omits. I, for one, will not quit
preaching them.

John, then, has his own ministry. Ninety-two per cent of his Gospel is his own. Look at his matchless fifteenth chapter. Take the shoes off your feet and enter the seventeenth chapter. John's business is to make majestically clear that Jesus Christ is the Son of God. And he does it! Here is his very first verse: "In the beginning was the Word [eternity], and the Word was with God [equality], and the Word was God [deity]."

Let me finish with two things: praise for the revelation this Gospel gives ("Thanks be unto God for his unspeakable gift"), and a prayer for my letter critic, "Lord, open the young man's eyes." Amen.

CHAPTER TEN

FOR WHOM THE BELL *NEVER* TOLLS

IN the long and twisted history of Homo sapiens, one of our matchless species has periodically felt himself born under a star of destiny which predestinated and dedicated him to a strange task. It was this—to be the undertaker to lay away with due reverence and suitable decorum the body of that "elect lady" known to us as the Church of Jesus Christ.

In the days of John Wesley, the brilliant Scottish philosopher, David Hume, and the vitriolic Frenchman, Voltaire, cheered each other along in this sobering task. It required some nerve to dig a grave large enough for this "lady" who is almost two millenniums old. The ordering of the service, the rehearsing of the requiem, and the inviting of guests for solemn mourning are not easy either! The tolling of the bell requires quite a little nerve, too.

But there is just one thing that is sternly required to make a funeral a real success—a corpse. Is the "elect lady" sick? weak? diseased? by schisms rent asunder?

Yes, this has been the Church over the centuries. But she is not dead. So if you are interested in prophecy (and even if you are not), let me tell you the "elect lady" will *never* die! She has an eternal content which is indestructible.

I suppose every ship at sea has an underwriter. That means that in case of loss, ship and cargo of any value are covered by a guarantor. Should the ship be wrecked, some corporation will pay in full for all damage to ship, cargo, and crew. Well, "the old ship of Zion" is blessedly and adequately underwritten. To be sure, as the buccaneers of old stopped the ships, massacred the crews, and stole the valued cargo, so at times the Church has been mutilated. (Talk of the Covenanters, and every true Scotsman is stirred; or think of the Huguenots in the seventeenth century; or remember the massacre of St. Bartholemew.) Yes, the Church has been violated and vivisected. Yet the Church never has nor ever will be finally vanquished. And what is the secret of her eternal youth? "Lo, *I am with you alway*, even unto the end of the age."

At this moment, as the power politicians and scientists play a fast and exciting game on the field of life, the Church *seems* sidelined, a mere watcher. But wait! The Church will renew her strength and come back under a super-anointing of the Spirit "fair as the moon, clear as the sun, and terrible as an army with banners." The Lord is coming back—not for a weary widow, nor for a sick Church languishing on a hospital bed—but for His bride. Usually a bride is radiant, full of life, overflowing with love, and blest to share the bounty of her husband. In view of this, I believe the Lord desires to rapture His Church in the full blaze of a Holy Ghost revival.

Coleridge the poet once began "playing" with drugs, assured in himself that he could remain their master; but they mastered him, "vitiated his vitality, snapped his will, and brought him to the grave a defeated husk, with the marrow of his genius dried in his brain." Even so, unless the Church of Jesus Christ awakens to her tremendous commission, mankind's toying with atomic power will spell doom for millions.

In the First World War, before Nurse Cavell was shot at her graveside, she said, "Patriotism is not enough." So let me say to those churches who are falsely contented that they are not liberal in doctrine but steadfast, busy with works, intolerant against the cults, and have "not fainted": "Orthodoxy is not enough!" The early church at Ephesus had these same qualifications (Rev. 2:2, 3), yet she heard the voice of the One walking in the midst of the seven golden candlesticks who said, "Thou art fallen." Think of it—with all that list of commendable attributes, f-a-l-l-e-n! God pity us today. We are as the Ephesians, and if we fail to function in the capacity for which the Lord has raised us up, we too are threatened with the removal of our candlestick.

But personally, I believe God, who says that in the last days (and we are in them) He will pour out of His Spirit (Joel 2:28–32). Note the "shalls" in this prophecy—not "could be" or "there is a possibility of," but the definite promise—"I *will* pour out my Spirit upon all flesh; and your sons and your daughters *shall* prophesy, your old men *shall* dream dreams, your young men *shall* see visions: and it *shall* come to pass, that whosoever *shall* call on the name of the Lord *shall* be delivered: for in Mount Zion and in Jerusalem *shall* be deliverance, as the Lord hath said, and in the remnant whom the Lord *shall* call."

Therefore, to whomsoever it may concern, desist from the repetitious folly of trying to bury the Church. At the moment she may be asleep, but watch out— she is going to wake, to war, to win! "Thanks be unto God who giveth us the victory."

> "So be it, Lord, Thy throne shall *never*,
> Like earth's proud empires, *pass away;*
> Thy kingdom stands and grows *forever*
> Till all Thy creatures own Thy sway."

CHAPTER ELEVEN

PAUL—BLESSED MAN !

IT was Wade Robinson who coined the phrase,

"Something lives in every hue
Christless eyes have never seen."

The Christless eyes of the scientist look on the ancient ruins of Philippi and see nothing there but a paradise for archeologists. The unillumined eyes of the historian look back to Philippi and remark on the fact that there Octavian and Mark Antony met Brutus and Cassius in battle and subdued them. But the anointed eyes of the Christian see Philippi as the place where the Apostle Paul established a bridgehead for the gospel of the grace of God in Europe.

When Paul arrived in Philippi, he had already been to Jerusalem, the capital city of the Jewish religion. He had stopped at Ephesus, the capital city of heathen religion; he was en route to Athens, the capital city of the intellectuals, and would finally finish his course in Rome, the capital city of military might. There, on his last missionary journey, he wrote his epistle to the people of Philippi, where he had first entered

Europe with the message of redeeming love. At the time of Paul's writing to the Philippians, he had notched twenty-three golden years of ministry all over Asia Minor. What a God-inspired ministry! Henry Varley's statement, "The world has yet to see what God can do through *one* man completely dedicated to Jesus Christ," may have been effective to challenge D. L. Moody, who was sitting there listening—but actually the statement is not true. One could list a hundred names, glorious names of outstanding men who in their day have turned the world upside down; and then when one has made the list, he could put Paul at the head of them all. It is said that a Chinaman wrote the Lord's Prayer on a grain of rice. That was wonderful. But there is something infinitely more wonderful: God crammed eternity and infinity and immensity into the heart of the Apostle Paul. Apart from the Son of God, Paul was the wealthiest man that ever lived (though the original John Rockefeller left more riches than any other living man and made Croesus look like an amateur at gathering wealth). What a legacy Paul left to the world! Down through the ages, millions of men and women, spiritually exhausted, have renewed their strength as they have read the mighty epistles of this colossus. Including the Epistle to the Hebrews, Paul wrote fourteen marvellous epistles. Yet after reading them all, one is impressed not by the cleverness of the remarkable thinker but by the courage of a remarkable leader.

It all began on the Damascus road when Saul carried beneath his toga what he considered to be the death certificate of the infant Church. Had Saul at that time met only a preacher and heard only a sermon, he might never have been heard of again. But Saul met Christ and heard His voice. Then when the fire-eating Pharisee, whose stormy soul was corroding with the acid of religious bitterness, was met by Deity, Saul was turned from darkness to light and from the power of Satan unto God. That day the history of man took a new turn. One can summarize Paul's spiritual transaction in this way:

It was an *exchanged* life—"Not I, but Christ."

It was an *expensive* life—He "suffered the loss of all things."

It was an *exciting* life—He "fought with wild beasts."

It was an *explicit* life—"This one thing I do."

It was an *exemplary* life—"What things you have seen and heard in me, do."

Paul had found rest—and yet he became the most restless man that ever lived. He had found joy—and yet he was in continual heaviness and sorrow of heart for the lost. He had found peace—but he waged an unending war against all the powers of darkness.

Self-abasement ("humble yourselves") is one thing; self-effacement ("not I but Christ") is entirely different. To the Philippians, Paul uttered what to me is one of the most daring things ever uttered by any man: that "Christ shall be magnified *in my body*, whether it be by life, or by death" (Phil. 1:20). Else-

where Paul said of the very people to whom he wrote
these words: "We were shamefully treated at Philippi" (backs torn till they had been like a plowed
field). Truly Paul bore in his body the marks (the
brands) of the Lord Jesus. Paul was like those escaped
slaves who had their hands and feet and backs branded
in the temple of Heracles. Henceforth Paul's hands,
feet, and mind were sanctified to the eternal purpose
of the fearless Prince of Peace.

Having presented his *own* body a living sacrifice,
Paul had authority for exhorting the Romans to do
likewise: "I beseech *you* . . . by the mercies of God,
that *ye* present *your* bodies a living sacrifice" (Rom.
12:1, 2). As someone has pointed out, to realize what
the mercies of God are, there is no need to go back
to sin's origin in the garden of Eden, but merely to
unveil the rebellious human heart in man, which is
set against the will and works of God, and loves darkness rather than light. (Read the first six chapters of
Romans.) It is the mercy of God that man can be
forgiven; it is the mercy of God that man can be re-
instated to be a son of God; it is the mercy of God
that man can be cleansed from his sin; it is the mercy
of God that man can be endued with power from on
high.

Paul, then, beseeches (the word is "I entreat; I
urge, or I beg"). He beseeches others to present themselves living sacrifices, holy, acceptable unto God (Rom.
12:1). Did this mean that they were to go to the altar
and dedicate *themselves? Can* you dedicate corrup-

tion? *Can* you dedicate carnality? When getting married, does a bridal couple take to the altar a filthy garbage can, overrunning with all the waste from the kitchen? Is it any less fitting for a man to present at God's altar all his corruption—his evil, his lust, jealousies, pride, bitterness and inflated ego? Do we present our bodies to be *made* holy? Do we not rather go first to the Cross for cleansing, and then present what we have as a living sacrifice? The Spirit-controlled tongue has *no* acid; the Spirit-controlled heart has *no* bitterness; the Spirit-controlled mind has *no* evil imaginations; the Spirit-controlled will lusteth *not* to envy; the Spirit-controlled affection knows *no* covetousness.

In the Old Testament, the offering was examined by the priest first; if it had blemishes, it was rejected. In the same way, unless there has been complete cleansing, I believe we can *not* present our entire being at the altar to be a living sacrifice. Likewise in the Old Testament, there was a set order for presenting offerings to God: the skin, the blood, the flesh, and the fat. And there is order also in the New Testament. Let the man who has had by the Spirit a revelation of his inward corruptions cleanse himself from these through the blood of Christ and through the baptism with the Holy Ghost and fire—and then present his cleansed heart and life at the feet of Jesus Christ to be a living sacrifice.

One of the poets captured the meaning of presenting ourselves to the Lord when he said, "That my

whole being may proclaim Thy being and Thy ways."
Another put it this way:

> "Let my hands perform His bidding,
> Let my feet run in His way;
> Let my eyes see Jesus only,
> Let my lips speak forth His praise.
> *All* for Jesus, all for Jesus."

Joachim Lange in about 1690 wrote,

> "O God, what offering shall I give to Thee,
> The Lord of earth and skies?
> My spirit, soul, and flesh receive,
> A holy, living sacrifice.
> Small as it is, 'tis all my store;
> More should'st Thou have if I had more."

Lord, may we be living sacrifices, "holy and acceptable unto God, which is [our] reasonable service."

CHAPTER TWELVE

AND HE PRAYED

THAT literary genius, Robert Louis Stevenson, though hounded by handicaps and pinioned with pain, turned tragedy into triumph. His battle with tuberculosis lasted years; then came the master stroke—blindness; later came sciatica with such an iron grip that the moving of a muscle was excruciating pain. In this derelict condition, Stevenson, the writer, was ordered to bed, and there the doctor strapped up his right arm to immobilize it. Writing meant agonizing pain. Days later the doctor came, only to be staggered at Stevenson's determination to work. The wellspring within was gushing forth. Then the doctor speculated, "Bitter things will be written and dark shadows of pain translated into verse." How wrong he was! Under this duress, the brilliant author of *Treasure Island* gave the world the glittering book, *A Child's Garden of Verse*. When a man can carry Stevenson's load and still sing, he is worthy of any man's admiration.

There is a parallel story in the Christian world. Its hero, too, was handicapped, for he had a close-range fight with the tubercular monster. This man polished no literary gems (though he was capable of it), produced no books, wrote no poems, built no church, and founded no society. About two hundred years ago he died. But today he lives, for from his innermost being there is still flowing a challenge to sacrificial and sustained prayer. This giant in the faith is, of course, David Brainerd.

John Wesley caught some heat from Brainerd and urged his brother Charles to see that every minister in Methodism in that day read Brainerd's unmatched diary. Jonathan Edwards unwittingly burned a part of Brainerd's classic record, but the remainder still carried fire. The Brainerd story touched Forbes Robertson of Brighton and moved him to eloquence. Dr. A. J. Gordon of Boston read the tale, trekked to Brainerd's grave in the snow, and there bowed his head. From then on Gordon's ministry was changed. William Carey of England, who was shaken after meditating on the devotion of the zealot, Brainerd, opened the gospel to the Orient. Henry Martyn, also of England (Smith prizeman at twenty-one and senior wrangler of his university), forsook his loved Lydia and went to India after the call of God came to him through reading the life story of our hero, David Brainerd. There in India Martyn completed the first New Testament translation in Arabic. Bishop French and Anthony Groves, John Wilson and George Maxwell Gordon were alike stirred by Brainerd's diary. After these facts, who can deny the profit of "the corn of wheat" that falls into the ground and dies?

Even now, two hundred years after Brainerd, men are still stirred and challenged by his life. Recently in the library of Princeton Seminary, I myself handled with affection the badgerskin-covered Hebrew lexicon that Brainerd carried with him on his famous crusade for the lost souls of the Indians. The volume itself seemed a challenge!

Here is my point: If *one* man could influence the Christian world as this man has done, what would an army like him do? There is no field more unexplored in Christian experience and possibility than this limitless field of prayer. Prayer means care for souls. Prayer means pain. Prayer means privacy, for often the battle is waged alone. Prayer means power. Prayer, Luther said, means "sweat on the soul." Prayer means filling in the sufferings of Christ. We cannot shoot fire-belching jet planes with sling shots nor repulse tanks with bottles; less still can we push back the powers of darkness with mere words. Jude talks of praying "in the Holy Ghost." This praying alone can bring to pass the purpose of a holy God and put to flight the army of alien powers. This praying is no toy soldier's game. This is realism. This is a fight to the death—*no* parley with the enemy—*no* truce—*no* terms—a fight *to the death!*

With some accuracy a recent writer portrayed the present, bleak picture of the slow-footed Church. Then to relieve the shadowy story, he grabbed the truth of Joel 2:28, "Afterwards, . . . I will pour out of my Spirit on all flesh," and hailed this truth as a picture of hope.

Indeed, such it is if not divorced from its context, for the *whole* of Chapter 2 of Joel is the pattern as a hand-maid to revival. This is a prescription for a sick church and for a dying world. God is a God of order, and the order is clear in the chapter mentioned. (The peril of all Bible teaching is that we get lopsided and, like Ephraim, get overdone on one side of our understanding and underdone on the other side.) Only they who fulfill God's commands have a full claim on the Lord.

As I see it, believers need a new concerted effort for this crucial hour. For far less worthy causes than this, we can dislocate our programs when it suits us so to do. Do men pass *forever* from eternal mercy? And is it true that there is *no* arbitration after the judgment seat of Christ? If you give a positive answer, then is there anything on earth worth more than the power of the Lord moving upon mankind? Though you cannot be the salt of the whole earth nor the light of the whole world, you may season your community and lighten your neighborhood. In the saintly Brainerd's dying moments, he passed on to the Church God's secret for revival in this or any other day. Listen to the pain-gasped word—travail, t r a v a i l, t-r-a-v-a-i-l. Let's try it!

CHAPTER THIRTEEN

THE CHURCH—A RECRUITING STATION

AT the call of presidents and premiers, men hasten to recruiting stations—careers forgotten, professions left, comforts forsaken, and homes deserted. As peril from the approaching enemy intensifies, weeping wives and sobbing sweethearts are tearfully left. Yet no one calls this folly. To shrink from this is cowardice; to rebel against the order smells of treachery. No mother warns her son of the stupidity of breaking off his university studies, even though he may return as a lifetime casualty—lamed, blinded, permanently crippled, or mentally unstable from enemy brainwashing. In the fight for freedom, this is all calculated and, to some degree, expected in the name of patriotism.

But what risks does the spiritual life offer? Note it carefully that it is *a liberal* at the Evanston Conference who has been left to deplore the easy way folk are accepted these days into the "church of the living God." This is an hour of anarchy in the world, of lawlessness in the Church. For everyone to do that which is "right in his own eyes" is thought to be democracy in the spiritual realm. But does democracy exist to the soldier? Can he fight when he wants, sleep when he likes, ground his plane according to fancy? Can the sailor speed to port when plagued with homesickness? No! The emotions must be mastered; iron must enter the will as well as the soul. The vision of lovely children must be forgotten and the enemy faced, so that later the soldier may return to family and freedom.

Summer sees Bible conferences in full swing, for which the Lord be praised; but what a fever of feasting on the book of Ephesians, with the accent on the first chapter (sharing with Christ) while almost skipping over the last chapter (fighting with Him)! There are many followers of the Lord these days. But how many are true disciples—disciplined ones? The very last thing that we tell new converts is that they are soldiers, called to orders, to arms, and to alms; that they are to be submissive to undershepherds; that they are not to be entangled with the affairs of this life; that they are to endure hardness, to espouse self-denial, and to glory (not just keep their chins up) in tribulation. Even at Bible conferences we cater to the youth of the day. Fellows old enough to face bloody battlefields on foreign shores are thought too immature to face hell's carnage on the home front (which in this case may be dope peddlers, stinking saloons, and vice on Main Street).

A flash-back in mind the other day staggered me with the realization that two and three hundred years ago there were spiritual giants in the earth. Men were mature at twenty-one years—had left college and university and were established as men with a message. See James Chalmers, the missionary-martyr of New Guinea, a full-blown preacher at nineteen. Consider Robert Murray McCheyne. At twenty-nine years of age he thrilled to say, "Farewell mortality; welcome eternity." A Dundee newspaper, paying tribute to his passing, said that in Robert McCheyne, Christ had walked those Scottish streets. A host of other giants-in-their-youth could be cited. But in this hour it is the hoary head that commands the pulpit.

Easy-going preachers produce easy-going believers. We have more star preachers than scarred preachers, more expositors than exposers, more who are concerned to "get it over" than to "pray it through." We have more religious educators than soul emancipators. The pulpiteer of our times is expected to enlighten the mind rather than to enliven the conscience. To many, the width of his head matters more than the depth of his heart. So, even with a steel ring of communism around the world, and the sewers of moral filth pouring over it, we find the Church more interested in pie than piety, and the Lord's weakened army "by schism rent asunder" and by conflicting interpretations oppressed.

On the contrary, let the Church become a recruiting booth. Youth likes a challenge. Where is there

more need or greater opportunity for courage than in
this battle of the Lord? This is a perpetual warfare.
Let there be no truce with this enemy, much less a
parley. The fight is on. The pressure increases. The
ranks are broken.

> "Ye that are men now serve Him
> Against unnumbered foes;
> Let courage rise with danger,
> And strength to strength oppose."

Let no man think of fighting hell's legions if he is
still fighting an internal warfare. Carnage without
will sicken him if he has carnality within. It is the
man who has surrendered to the Lord who will never
surrender to his enemies.

One great risk in praying is that sometimes God
takes us at our word. Then will come the test. I am
amazed that men, who at the call of their nation lov-
ingly kiss their wives and leave home possibly for
years, shrink back at the call of Christ. For natural
warfare men will leave home for years, but to fight
against principalities and powers, they cannot leave
home one night a week for the church prayer meeting! Shivering and foodless, men will lie for nights in
bloody, muddy trenches; or lie in a ditch after bailing
out from a plane; or, chilled to the spine, hold on to
a spar for hours in a freezing ocean—yet find it almost impossible to spend a half night in a warm
church praying.

Is the fact not this, that we have underestimated
the total war to which the devil has committed his

horde of demons and men alike? Is it not true that cataracts have formed over our eyes (maybe with watching too much T.V.) so that we have completely misjudged the horror of that eternal hell to which at this moment millions of souls are marching? Does such a picture stir your soul and stab your conscience? Are you sleeping at the price of another's peril? Recently, when a hunting dog ferreted into a pile of rocks and was trapped, men fought with cold, rain, and fatigue for two days and nights to find the entombed dog. Are not men more than dogs? Will men be entombed in hell forever because you were playing instead of praying?

A coroner once exonerated a man who said he had swung his lamp at the level crossing as a driver sped toward the oncoming express and was killed, but later he confided to a friend that he had had no light in his lamp. Friend, in the gross darkness that has overcome this generation, are you swinging the lamp of an empty profession?

CHAPTER FOURTEEN

LORD, LET ME DIE CLIMBING!

ON this side of eternity there is no finality to Christian experience. Certainly "if we walk with the Lord in the light of His Word, *what a glory He sheds on our way!*" In the light of Jesus' glory and grace, the things of God become strangely clear. Though there are many adversaries, glorious peaks of revelation *can* be scaled by the ardent soul. But even so, heaven has not yet issued credit cards for grace. There is a price to be paid for spiritual growth. As long as we tread this terrestrial ball, none can say in matters of spiritual travel, "I have arrived." Our spiritual horizons are ever receding.

Today an itch for "things" has spread a foul restlessness among believers, for we are victims of competitive living. There is more anxiety about how to make a living than about how to live. But suppose that John Jones does get a Cadillac as long as a city block, and then suppose his aunt dies and leaves him a half million dollars so that he can live in Florida and have a super-home, with servants in attendance.

Has *that* added a cubic foot to his spiritual stature? In the categories of the spiritual, does he rate higher because of his social climb? Does the extra tithe that he may give to the church assure him of a back-door access to divine favors? Can gifts of the Spirit be received with the gold of Ophir? Will the mayor's chain about his neck mean that there are open to him spiritual resources denied to Jimmy James, who at this moment is sweating at a furnace in a Pittsburgh steel mill? To all these questions my heart replies, "Be it far from Thee, Lord, to do these things." If then, pearls, power, and prestige do not inch us nearer the secrets of the Most High, why not treat them but dung so that we may win Christ? I am almost terrified at the thought of the judgment bar of God for the modern close-to-earth Christians (not that the writer or anyone else has received a free pass for that great day).

Everywhere folk are crying out against this treadmill existence of so-called modern life, for too often those who do not bear the brand of Cain bear the brand of boredom. Yet God is longing—let me repeat— *God is longing* to sweep rivers of grace through the deserts of our parched spirituality.

At the beginning of this chapter we said that there is no finality to spiritual living this side of eternity. There may have been a complete yielding to Christ many years ago, and since that day not a thing taken from the altar. But the acid test is this: What have I brought to the altar since then? In the things of the

kingdom, progress is not automatic, for a man may be
only fifty *weeks* old in grace, even though he was
saved fifty *years* ago. Maturity in grace has nothing
to do with years but rather with prayerful obedience
to the revealed will of God. In a day when the cry of
"Grace! Grace! Free grace!" has been overdone, we
sound like a heretic to say that in the spiritual life
there are things that can be bought. But listen to the
Lord Jesus himself speak: "I counsel thee to *buy* of
me" (Rev. 3:18); and Paul agrees by saying, "*Buy
up* the opportunity" (Eph. 5:16, R.V.). But how?

Tonight I go to a friend's house and sit in pleasant
fellowship and edifying conversation. "I shall not stay
long," I say. But how the time slips by! It is getting
near midnight. Now at last I am home, tired and
sleepy. Then I pause to reflect for a moment: I gave
my friend four hours of my time, yet my devotions
took less than one hour; therefore, I prefer time with
godly people more than time with God himself.

Or look at that courting couple. They leave the
comfort and warmth of home to walk down a lane in
biting frost. Why? Well obviously because they are
in love and want each other far more than creature
comforts. Is human love greater than divine love? In
matters of the Spirit, is fellowship *about* the Father
better than fellowship *with* the Father?

To go to the Cross for "life" in regeneration and
for "death" in sanctification is fine. But even in these
Christian experiences there is no finality. I mean that

there is a daily dying. If I today deny myself something that I want (or even feel that I need), I have
not thereby merited heaven; but by denying myself
something and by channeling that money for the
cause of lost souls, I have proven that my actions
are related to my theology. If God is going to increase
in my life, then somebody is going to decrease in it.
If I am bent on spiritual maturity, then I must see
God more, and that means I am going to see others
less. If I am not going to be "ashamed at his coming" (the very tone of I John 2:28 suggests that some
will want to hide), then I must pursue my high calling of God in Christ with diligence. There is no es-
calator to the beckoning peaks of spiritual vision.

In conclusion, let each of us pray, "Lord, it is
truly a good, stiff climb, but 'plenteous grace with Thee
is found.' Yet, can two walk together, Lord, except
they be agreed? Lord, I agree; help Thou me to die
climbing."

CHAPTER FIFTEEN

INSPIRED UTTERANCE

THE famed Irish evangelist, W. P. Nicholson, autographed his photographs with John 3:30, "He must increase, but I must decrease." In his letters he used to "tail off" with "Yours, till hell freezes," and then came his name. For some years, in like manner, I have added the reference Ephesians 6:19 to my own private letters with the hope that the recipient would lay hold of the word *utterance.*

Now in this verse Paul was asking prayer "that utterance may be given." On his own admission he was no orator. In his mental scrap with the intellectuals on Mars' Hill, he heard the wise men ask, "What will *this babbler* say?" (Acts 17:18). "His letters, they say, are weighty and strong; but his bodily presence is weak, and *his speech of no account*" (II Cor. 10: 10). Paul could have omitted this slight to himself, but he cheerfully states both their contempt for his scarred body and also their low rating of his speech.

But these facts alone do not explain his plea to the Ephesians for utterance. Nor is he thinking here

of tongues, the utterance given on the day of Pentecost. He is rather thinking of authority. For instance,
in writing me awhile ago, Dr. Paul Rees mentioned
that in his last meeting his preaching had a new sense
of authority. Authority, I believe, is what the Apostle
meant by utterance. Then one other day while praying with two brothers in Christ, one of them began to
plead with God that we might have utterance. Again
the word utterance gripped my heart.

Jesus had utterance. When officers returning from
Jesus to the Pharisees said of the Master, "Never man
spake like this man," they were not referring to eloquence or wisdom. Again, in Gethsemane, officers
from the chief priests were unable to arrest the de-
fenseless Son of God because He had an authority.
He simply said, "I am he," and men fell as if smitten
by lightning. I believe a transmission of power from
His very lips slew those men. Even His critics said,
"He speaks as one having authority and not like [those
windbags] the scribes" (Matt. 7:29).

A man can transmit his thinking to the mind of
another by knowledge, coupled with the wave lengths
of speech; but by knowledge alone he cannot convey
his feelings. For instance, the effects of a cry of a
baby at midnight may be varied. It may create compassion in the heart of the mother, but at the very
same time it may cause nothing but consternation in
the mind of the man next door who is trying to get
to sleep. Even as the effect of human thinking on another human can be disastrous, interpretations of

Scripture on the merely intellectual level can be equally disrupting. But, *the authority of the Spirit* on God's messenger will create clear understanding in the mind of the hearer, for the Holy Spirit is not the author of confusion.

Here, then, is the core of what I am trying to say: The Psalmist cried in Psalm 51:15, "O Lord, open thou my lips." Was he dumb? No! Could he not open his own mouth? Yes! This was not a problem of face but of force. Matthew 5:1 states that the Saviour "opened his mouth and taught them." The Master promised that those who followed Him should also have this experience, for "it is not ye that speak, but the Spirit of your Father which speaketh in you."

Let me give you several examples of utterance: First, a surging crowd of priests, of partisans, and of persecutors alike thronged to hear John the Baptist. They were not magnetized by miracles. As offended as they were deserted, the hierarchy asked, "Who art thou?" (I guess there was emphatic disdain in the voice.) Then the Spirit-filled John the Baptist answered, "I am a voice." He knew that he had utterance.

At Pentecost this utterance was upon the men who, Spirit-generated, streamed out of the Upper Room with woeful utterance to the mingling masses. The record reads, "When the listeners heard this, they were pricked in their hearts." Only Spirit-inspired utterance could cause such soul-anxiety.

Later, when the Spirit-born, Spirit-filled, and Spirit-anointed Stephen spake in the great synagogue of the Libertines, Cyrenians, and Alexandrians, and a sprinkling of folk from Cilicia and Asia, the record reads, "They were not able to resist the wisdom and the Spirit by which he spake." Stephen had utterance.

Again, consider the following incident: Jock Purves, a beloved Scotchman (he wrote two books on his people), once told me he thought the greatest thing that John Knox ever did was to dismiss his congregation one morning in St. Giles Cathedral because he had no message for them. Most of us would have warmed up an old sermon or stammered through a few scattered thoughts. But *Knox wanted utterance.*

Finally, the story is told of a young minister who once had to substitute for a more famous colleague—always an unenviable task. When the people were asked what they thought of the unnamed herald, one of them replied criptically, "I have often heard a better preacher, but I have never heard a preacher better." Evidently that messenger had utterance.

Pray for me that "utterance may be given me that I may open my mouth boldly, to make known the mystery of the gospel." May God give back to us preaching with authority.

CHAPTER SIXTEEN

HALF ALIVE?

THE paradox of the Bible is this: At the same time it is the most comforting and the most discomforting book in the world. It lifts up the lowly and casts down the proud. The Word succors the suffering as a mother hugs a weeping child; but it also slaps us in the face. It says those who are alive are dead, but those who are dead "in Christ" are alive. This Wonder Book repels men, yet it draws men. It offers men hope, yet it casts them into despair. It says men who have everything have nothing, yet those who have nothing (but Christ) have everything. It declares that men who say they "know" do not know, and that men who the world says know nothing can triumphantly say, "We *know* that we have passed from death unto life."

Imagine an exclusive party in the Waldorf Astoria Hotel—the company liberally garnished with millionaires, stars, and the elite of the land. Suddenly, a prophet-like man grabs a chair, stands on it, and with a trumpet voice calls, "She that liveth in pleasure

is dead while she liveth!" Can you imagine the visible
reaction to that utterance? Can you see this man
sprawling on the sidewalk, after having been "thrown
out on his ear"? But is it really wild talk, a bit of
religious random, and a frank overstatement to say
these glittering ladies are just dressed-up death?
Is it just religious rudeness to say that these tycoons
and Wall Street wallahs are "dead in sin"? The answer is this: "To the law and to the testimony: if
they speak not according to this word, it is because
there is no light in them" (Isaiah 8: 20). "What saith
the scriptures?" For instance, look at these words:
"This my son was *dead* and is alive again"; "You hath
he quickened who were *dead* in trespasses and sins."
The complaint of the Christ was "Ye will not come
unto me that ye might have life." Clearly this implies
that at that moment they were dead.

Today the highway of natural life is crowded with
people who have no spiritual life. They have *natural*
life and keep living by regular meals; they have *intellectual* life and keep their thinking alive with information; they have *emotional* life and are satisfied
by manifesting their love; they have *social* life and
attempt to keep up with the Joneses; they have *business* life and pursue it with diligence. But yet, none
other than H. G. Wells declared, "There is a God-
shaped blank within each one of us." How true!
There is within us an area that remains a vacuum
forever unless the Spirit of God comes to indwell us.
So we are faced with the given fact that we *are* living among the dead!

I do not wonder the suicide rate is so high. I marvel it is so low. Where are men going? Is Dr. J. S. Stewart right in saying that modern man is staggering between Vanity Fair and Armageddon? I think he is. This dead world needs *life*. The Bible is *a book* of life. In the Bible there is *a tree* of life in the first book, and *a river* of the water of life in the last book. And the whole book is *the history* of life. It reveals the life of God for the dead soul of man. In a vilipending, incisive phrase that should shake us, Walter Lippmann speaks of the Church as a group of "grimly spiritual persons devoted to the worship of sonorous generalities." Isn't that delicious? Rather—it sets my teeth on edge!

Charles Haddon Spurgeon said of the mighty George Whitefield, "HE LIVED. [The capitals are Spurgeons!] Other men seem to be only half alive; but Whitefield was all life, and fire, and wing, and force." He is speaking there of a man "full of faith and of the Holy Ghost." Is the world "dead" today because we as believers are only half alive? The degree of life in the Church determines the degree of death in the world.

In a great student meeting in Edinburgh, Henry Drummond read a letter from a man who had made utter shipwreck of life. It was full of bitterness, acrimony, and bewilderment—a graphic revelation of a sin-sunk and ruined soul, and was signed, "Thanatos" (the Greek word for death)! Drummond declared that if he had ever thought any man beyond redemption,

it was that man. About two years later, there was another night when Drummond again had his worshipping students in their hundreds at his feet. "Gentle-
men," he cried, "I have had a letter from 'Thanatos,'
that moral, social, and spiritual wreck that I told you
of." Then he added triumphantly, "He has passed
from death unto life; Christ has changed him." Hal-
lelujah! What a Saviour!

David Garrick, that prince of character actors, is
said to have so identically portrayed certain people
that he seemed a living incarnation of them. However,
the story goes that one night Garrick was unmoved
and unmoving, obviously uninspired and lethargic.
Then suddenly there was an unexpected and dramatic
twist in his interpretation. Again he was re-living
a person in history.

"How do you account for the change?" asked one
critic of another. "Why did he suddenly catch fire?"

"I espied Lord Chesterfield enter by the stage door,"
said the second critic, "and Garrick saw him too. From
that moment he became another man."

So when a man—any man—lets Christ enter his
life, he becomes *another man,* for " if any man be in
Christ, he *is* a new creature." Into his life comes the
life of God. That man lives life with a capital L.

CHAPTER SEVENTEEN

JOLT THE SLEEPING CHURCH

IT is well for us to remember that Jesus had scorching words of rebuke in His day for those who were able by the skies to read the coming storms and yet were blind to the signs of the times. Can we read the signs of *our* times? The hourglass of our dispensation is running out, and our skies glow crimson with the threatening storm of world distress. Four peaks stand out clearly: *spiritual lassitude*—with millions who profess Christ's name sleeping at the post of duty; *political servitude*—with millions crushed under the heel of communism; *scientific aptitude*—with millions of dollars spent on man-killing, earth-scorching devices; *moral turpitude*—with millions being spent on anti-crime efforts, etc.

The first of these factors engages us here—*spiritual lassitude*. In a moment of bitter self-reproach, Anatole France, the French critic, novelist, and satirist, said, "I have spent my life twisting dynamite into curling papers." What an imaginative yet disturbing phrase! What this statement meant in Anatole France's case, I do not know. But lay at *our* door as believers that charge of "twisting dynamite into curling papers," and it means we are deliberately mishandling God's "exceeding great and precious promises." For my part, what I *have* done in the past troubles me no more, for it is repented of and mercifully put under the blood of Christ; but what I have *not* done troubles me.

The dynamite in my hands is the infallible Word of the living God. No right-thinking Christian can doubt that the most urgent need of the hour is that we get this dynamite, this everlasting truth, carefully detonated beneath present-day easy believeism and jolt the sleeping Church into a mass attack against invading iniquity. Some strange twists are put on texts these days. Many think that a payment of tithes and once-a-week church attendance are the full requirements of the Lord. The over-preached idea of a Christian's sonship (the Lord of glory heavily obligated to meet His child's every prayer-whim) may delight some but is doping most. If God is so obligated, then are not we obligated also?

And now, *moral turpitude*. The appalling arrogance of sin is most disturbing. Make no mistake. Iniquity does not slink any more along a side street with its head down, but rather swaggers down Main Street. Neither does iniquity cover its poison as in the days of yore, but openly defies the old standards and mocks the "Mother Grundy" mind of morals.

For an eye opener on the youth side of sin, here is a passage from a modern writer. She says that mixed

bathing in the raw at midnight is done in many of the
warm lakes in America. A fellow-traveller of hers adds,
"I have written endless pages of sentimental slush because the wages of sin is a check from an editor. I have
sinned on paper more than Mephisto himself. I have
done more severe penance on paper than the most de-
vout Trappist monk. My conscience has been purged,
calcimined, and resurrected at least three times a week.
I have sinned and sinned. . . . I sit on a throne em-
broidered with rehearsed sins. I shake consciences out
of my sleeve."

A publishing company of a best seller offers a
book with the swash-buckling affront, "This book is
so outspoken that the federal government has twice
tried to ban it from the country." One stops only to ask,
Why does a government try and not succeed? If the
same government knew where men were making rivers of moonshine whiskey, would they merely *try*
to stop the business and quit without "mopping up"?
Is the zeal merely that the government is cheated of
taxes? Are the lives of millions of unspoiled youth not
worth the banning by force of this vile literature (if
literature it can be called)?

If you think all this is the Sunday-school-teacher
attitude to modern trash, then listen to William Allen
White, who, after reading one of these lurid fiction sin-
breeders, said, "Seventy-two seductions in one book is
too much!" One deplores that there is never a word of
condemnation of immoral life, no disapproval of the
scoffing at religion, no shame at the scornful ridicule

of the sanctity of marriage, no contrition for misdeeds, no penalty for debauchery, not even remorse. Rather, halcyon days are offered and fiery experiences guaranteed for pre-marital or extra-marital love.

This whole mess of corruption is garnished by a faultless presentation of dazzlingly beautiful imagery, a masterpiece of adroit craftsmanship. This foul witches' brew of distorted standards and tempting iniquity is served in liberal portions in the pulp magazines of the hour. Young minds, unprepared by prayerful parents and ignorant of family altars, are being twisted, corrupted, and implanted with the seed of hell from the hands of money-hungry writers. Let the writers of these trash-can smut magazines know that they will help their nation's fall more quickly than will communistic philosophy!

Let me crown this sewer stuff with a statement from a Washington newspaperman: "I am alarmed at the truly extraordinary extent to which the country is drenched by the steadily increasing stream of pornographic periodicals and dirty fiction magazines. The plain truth is that in the matter of literary lewdness, we have taken the lead. . . . We were accustomed to marvel that another civilized country could openly permit the sale of such filth."

Christian parents, teachers, Christians en masse, stop! Scrutinize! Analyze! Check the reading matter of your children! Why not protest the pornographic magazines on the sales counters of the shops in your town?

In this evil hour, sin-bound, self-bound, hell-bound men and women must see again a great sin-convicting, soul-saving revival before the Lord comes!

"O God, give us more men aflame for Thee!—men sick of the monopoly of the devil here and everywhere else; men with burning hearts, brimming eyes, and bursting lips; men who fear nothing but sin, love nothing but Thy supreme will, desire nothing but to die that other men might live. Holy Father, I ask Thee in Jesus' Name to give us these men, lest the Church continue to drift farther and farther from the norm as revealed in The Acts of the Apostles. O Lord, awake us, lest we finally have to confess, 'I spent my lifetime twisting dynamite into curling papers'!"

CHAPTER EIGHTEEN

ON MEDITATION

THERE are times when things totally irrelevant
to spirituality become our schoolmaster to bring
us to Christ. For instance, what do you think a stark-
naked tree with a withered-looking arm limply grasp-
ing the sky has to do with the salvation of a man's
soul? In the sixteenth century such a tree challenged
Brother Lawrence, the Carmelite monk. First he
thought the tree dead; on second thought he remembered it was taking its winter nap and would resurrect
again. Then his thought turned inward: Would not
he too die? Would not he too have a resurrection?
The ultimate in his reflections led to a personal surrender to God, then a walk with Him. This culmin-
ated in writing his masterly little book, *The Practice
of the Presence of God*, which has literally sold into
millions of copies. Yet it all began with a withered-
looking tree.

In reading part of an old sermon by F. W. Robertson of Brighton, England, challenge came my way.
The noted minister is flinging the world and its

treasures at the feet of us all. He says, "These treasures are there *for the taking*," and then adds, "Do you wish to master any science or accomplishment? *Give yourself to it*, and it will be beneath your feet. Time and pains will do anything, for this world is given as the prize for men in earnest." F. W. Robertson has of course this Scripture to guide him in all this: "*Whatsoever* a man soweth, *that* shall he also reap" (Gal. 6:7).

To operate this law of success, one requirement among others is meditation. This is not to be confused with reverie—more commonly called daydreaming. Meditation is no vague, lay-in-the-field-on-your-back attitude, watching the clouds scurry by. That may be rest, but it is not meditation—it is mere passivity. Meditation is active. In the midst of tremendous activity, it may be that a provocative thought will demand withdrawal for contemplation and meditation if one is to get the full reward of a seed thought. To quote F. W. Robertson again: "Meditation is a state partly passive and partly active. Whoever has pondered long over a plan that he is anxious to accomplish, yet without at first seeing the way distinctly, knows what meditation is. The subject matter presents itself spontaneously in leisure moments; then all this sets the mind at work—contriving, imagining, rejecting, modifying. It is in this way that one of the greatest of English engineers, a man uncouth and unaccustomed to regular discipline of mind, is said to have accomplished his most marvellous triumphs. He threw bridges over almost impracticable torrents and also pierced the eternal mountains for his viaducts. Sometimes difficulties brought all the work to a pause. Then he would shut himself up in his room, eat nothing, speak to no one, and abandon himself intensely to the contemplation of that on which his heart was set. But at the end of two or three days he would come forth serene and calm, walk over to the place of difficulty, and quietly give orders which seemed the result of superhuman intuition. This was meditation."

Does not this illustration prove that "the children of this world are wiser in their generation than the children of light"? This engineer was a man fasting from food, from drink, and from fellowship with men. Rather than submit to some baffling obstacle of nature, he shut himself up to silent meditation, oblivious of praise or blame from others.

Repeatedly the Psalmist says, "I will meditate in thy precepts." Paul urges Timothy, his son in the gospel, to "meditate upon these things" (I Tim. 4:15). Just as a sentry would search a suspect who wanted to cross a national boundary, so meditation means to throw a roadblock across the mind and not let the thought go past until it has been thoroughly searched. In the language of the old proverb—"Squeeze the lemon dry"—a word or thought should be "held" until it can yield no more, at least for the time being.

Seeds buried with Tutankhamen, Egyptian king about 1400 B.C., were still fertile when Howard Carter found them in A.D. 1922. A little later, in a suitable atmosphere they sprang to life. Thoughts are like that. Bring them off the main street of the mind into the warm, cultivating atmosphere of prayerful meditation, and they will yield fruit unto life eternal.

Recently we heard of a believer who complained that private devotions were dry even though day by day he had risen early and read many chapters of the Scriptures. Another man told me that though he was reading ten chapters each morning, he was getting little soul sustenance from doing so. The source of that problem is easy—there had been no real meditation. Nowadays, who knits his own stockings or bakes his own bread? These arts are dying fast, though when some of us were young, they were respected greatly in our homes. One might ask, too, who bakes his own spiritual bread these days? There are so many aids to devotion, so many daily Scripture readings. The table is spread for us, but it lacks something. Spartan children were said to have been refused breakfast unless they had some sweat on the brow from hard industry. I wonder: Does the Lord bless most those who *dig* the most, who *meditate* the most, and therefore *get* the most, and *praise* the most? Asked what he thought was wrong with modern man, Albert Schweitzer replied tersely, "He can't think!" Think he's right?

> " 'Within the veil': Be this belov'd thy portion,
> Within the secret of thy Lord to dwell,
> Beholding Him until thy face His glory,
> Thy life His love, thy lips His praise shall tell."

CHAPTER NINETEEN

FROM THE BELLY OF HELL I CRIED

J ONAH'S extremity was God's opportunity! Jonah had the weeds about him and the waves above him. His jail house was a whale house, settled amid the roots of the mountains and chained in the dark waters of the Mediterranean Sea by the pillars of the earth. He had never read (or else had forgotten) that "if I make my bed in hell, thou art there," and that God's voice can reach to the uttermost part of the earth. All this he learned the hard way. Jonah was not in the belly of hell because of faith or fate or fortuitous circumstances, but as a result of planned evasion of the known will of God. There is this, too— God had His hand over it all.

Before we begin any application, look at this skeleton outline: "The Lord *sent out* a great wind," says the Authorized Version, or as old Miles Coverdale says, "The Lord *hurled out* a great storm into the sea." So then:

The Lord *prepared* the storm (1:4)
The Lord *prepared* a great fish (1:17)

The Lord *prepared* a gourd (4:6)
The Lord *prepared* a worm (4:7)
The Lord *prepared* a wind (4:8)

Concerning Jonah, verse three of chapter one says, "So he paid the fare." At Joppa, Jonah slipped the price of a ticket to Tarshish over the counter to the booking clerk. Most likely he paid it in a coin with a superscription of Jeroboam II. But no shipping clerk, nor even the rebel revivalist himself, knew the real price of that ticket—souls of men, and the anguish of a first submarine journey in a nightmarish experience on a foam-blubber bed in the whale's belly. (The judgment day alone will reveal the total fallacy of backsliding and the wretched cost of evading the will of God.) Jonah paid the fare in the coinage of pain, of privation, of peril, and finally of a prison in the depths of the sea. He cut himself off from God, and he cut men off from himself. He was useless to men and to God. (This is the dire peril of the backslider who is the devil's best friend.)

Having blinded his eyes to God's way, Jonah now closes his ears to God's voice. Notice that every movement is downward—he went *down* to Joppa, *down* into the side of the ship, *down* to the bottoms of the mountains. Every move of a backslider is always down, away from God.

His soul seared with disobedience, Jonah now falls asleep, even while the ship rolls in the trough of the storm and men cry out in fear. What a picture Jonah is of the sleep-snared believers of this hour! Was the world ever so rocked as now? Was the Church ever more sound asleep? I have not yet heard that a night of prayer has been staged for the agony of the Communist-castigated Congo. There has been more anger than agony over the crisis in Cuba. Millions of Chinese and others are literally perched on the tip of little Hong Kong, where incredible suffering reigns, malnutrition stalks, and suicide slays many. River boats crowd the shores, and children are born in conditions only rats should know—all this plus the fact that most of these millions are as far from God as Satan is from sainthood. But frankly, who cares? Whose business is it? A well-documented film of the refugee plight in Formosa or Hong Kong will be a tear-jerker for a few moments; then we roll over and snore! (The Septuagint Version adds that phrase, "Jonah snored"!)

Recently the perky, proud prince of Communist protagonists steamed his way to New York, and his gilt-edged cards asked Tito, Castro, and Nasser to the party. Never has such an evil brood descended on America. They came to plan division on a piece of land dedicated to unite the nations, as well as to plot slavery for an organization dedicated to freedom. They walked into America's front parlor to spawn their hell-conceived litters. No good can come out of evil men and evil plans.

Can hope be born in this hopeless mess? Can dedicated slaves plan to set men free? That U.N. confer-

ence, despite Khrushchev's transforming himself as the
dove of peace, might be listed as the most momentous meeting ever held since vile men plotted the death
of the Son of God. Unborn generations might live to
curse this Nasser-Tito-Castro-Khrushchev meeting. Just
what will set the emergency alarm of the Church ring-
ing? What can disturb this sleep of death? Will
America have to bow the knee to a dictatorship before she learns to bow the knee to God?

The present condition of Communist-controlled
China is sad beyond words, but it leaves a still more
bitter taste to remember that in the early centuries
of the Christian era, missionaries of the Nestorian
Church prodded into the heart of the Gobi desert, con-
quering the great mountains in their path and ulti-
mately establishing in China the Church of Jesus
Christ. By the eighth century there were bishoprics
in China and multitudes of Christians. Then came in-
difference along with compromise. Preachers began to
conciliate the Confucian scholars and to by-pass the
offence of the Cross. Then faded the Church. Sleep
came over her, and finally death, with inestimable
millions lost to the cause of Christ.

The panic-stricken sailors looked for a cause in
their storm. The captain settled on Jonah with the
cry, "What meanest thou, O sleeper? arise, call upon
thy God. . . . What is thine occupation? . . . What is thy
country? and of what people art thou?" Well might an
angry, fear-gripped, storm-tossed world look at a sleepy,

backslidden Laodicean Church and ask us what is our
business. Jonah did not call upon his God there. He
needed further humiliation; he must descend into the
belly of hell. From what must have seemed the point
of no return, and in the blackness and foulness of
the fish's inwards, Jonah made his prayer. Will God
have to allow the free nations the black bondage of
an evil oppressor before we really get serious about
a genuine Holy Ghost revival? Would the twin evils
of inflation and invasion be an adequate pincer movement to nip off the financial and lethargic chains that
fetter the indifferent Church? I am aware, of course,
that some have drugged themselves with what seems
a comfort—namely, they have been taught that before the roof falls in on America or Britain, there
will be a selective rapture to snatch us darling Christians from the paw of "the beast" or the power of the
"false prophet." One wonders, then, why the Lord
did not snatch the praying Koreans, and the conse-
crated Chinese, and genuine Christians in Germany
from the agony that they still endure.

A lady with firsthand information of the Hong
Kong situation says hungry children will dive for
even a thrown-out banana skin or orange peel. Who
can deny that today, from the belly of a hundred
Communist hells, millions are crying out to the Lord?
I remind you again, my comfortable Christian friend,
that out of their bondage, sorrow, and night, millions
are crying to the Lord of Sabbaoth for that relief
which supernatural power alone can bring. Just what
is the Lord (who prepared the fish, and the wind,

along with the worm and the gourd) preparing for us? Shall we cry only from the belly of hell?

The cause of this plight of the preacher Jonah was this: he was huffed because the Lord was going to pour out of His Spirit upon a heathen people. But Jonah hated Nineveh with a perfect hatred. Is it reasonable, thought Jonah, for me to cry to a hundred and twenty thousand souls to repent when all the time I know in my heart they will hearken to my cry? Wouldn't I lose face with Israel? Further, wasn't Nineveh predestined and prepared and prophesied of God to be the fast-coming scourge and the cruel prison-house of the conquered and captive Israel? Gladly, therefore, would Jonah have prophesied doom for Nineveh—but prophesy mercy? That was more than Jonah could take. Later, when Jonah had actually fulfilled his mission to Nineveh, you would have thought that the heart of the prophet would have leaped for joy because of Nineveh's repentance and because it shrouded man and beast in sackcloth and proclaimed a fast for men and dumb beast. But Jonah was mad! (Don't take my word for it; see chapter four, verse one: "It displeased Jonah exceedingly and he was very angry.") Ah, as far as Jonah was concerned it would be better that the Ninevites should perish in hell than that they should repent and have the smile of God upon them at a time when Israel was continuing in backsliding. Besides, so ignorant were the Ninevites that they could not discern between their right hand and their left!

In spiritual matters is there less stupidity abroad in the world today? Are we as afraid that Russia might have a Holy Ghost revival as Jonah was that Nineveh would have one? Can you remember the last time you heard a weeping intercessor pleading for the blind millions of sovietized sinners? One would imagine that the Lord's mercy for Russia had clean gone forever. God give Russia a John the Baptist, a Luther, a Knox, or a Wesley, to provoke us to call upon Him from the horrible pit of spiritual destitution, broken sabbaths, packed jails, and millions of divorce-devastated homes. Revival at any price? Others differ with me here, but I believe the Lord wants His Church to be a glorious Church, triumphant in a wave of revival so that she shall not be ashamed at His appearing. Revival is worthwhile at any price. But what a terrible price if we have to say as did Jonah, "My prayer came in unto thee, into thy holy temple . . . out of the belly of hell"!

CHAPTER TWENTY

CONSCIENCE DID IT!

THE ancients used to talk of a gold ring that had the appearance of any other ring, yet differed in at least this quality—the wearer, should he brood over an evil thought or contemplate an evil deed, would feel the ring pressing hard upon his finger.

Each of us has within us a thing still more wonderful—a thing that registers the approach of moral danger, or the transgression of known standards of uprightness. This is conscience. Milton wrote his famous *Paradise Lost* after he was married, and penned *Paradise Regained* after his wife died. In *Paradise Lost* you might recall that Milton puts these words into the mouth of the Creator concerning His creation: "I will put mine umpire in his breast." That is probably the best and the shortest definition of conscience ever made. An umpire, the dictionary says, is "the one called upon to decide, to choose, or to enforce rules." Isn't that just the ministry of conscience within us?

In his clever book, *The Critique of Pure Reason,*
Immanuel Kant says that two things filled him with
awe: one, the starry heavens; two, conscience in the
breast of us mortals. Unquestionably, conscience is our
trustworthy teacher, our faithful friend, and our care-
ful counsellor. William Shakespeare recites in *Hamlet*
(Act III),

"Thus conscience does make cowards of us all."

Then in *King Richard* (Act V) Shakespeare says,

"My conscience hath a thousand several tongues,
And every tongue brings in a several tale;
And every tale condemns me for a villain."

And Shelley called it thus: "Conscience—that undy-
ing serpent." This gets to a debatable point. Does
conscience ever die? I think not. We may ill-treat it,
dull it, sear it, or drown it; but it kicks back. Times
are when this thing within the breast is eloquent. One
day it seems to excuse. But the next day, with mur-
derous accuracy, it accuses.

If you talked of conscience in certain circles today, men would lift an eyebrow. They think of it
as a spare part, like the appendix. Some want to believe that at last men have "grown up," and therefore have outgrown this primary instinct. Howbeit,
the generation that "looks down its nose" at an old-
fashioned thing like the conscience has itself invented
a lie detector. That is almost too funny for words.

Millions of people in thousands of churches have
repeated hundreds of times, "suffered under Pontius

Pilate," thus commemorating the great battle with
his conscience that that proud embarrassed Roman
had.

What made Adam say, "I was afraid"? *Conscience did it!* What made Ahab say, "Hast thou
found me, O mine enemy?" *Conscience did it!* What
made David cry, "Have mercy upon me, O God"?
Conscience did it! What made Pilate's wife write,
"Have nothing to do with this just man"? *Conscience
did it!* What made Felix tremble? *Conscience did it!*
What made Judas wail, "I have betrayed innocent
blood"? *Conscience did it!*

Today, too, men still battle with this inward monitor. They put it to sleep with some slick drug, but it
wakes with a louder cry. They slay it, only to find
it has a resurrection. They laugh and joke at it in the
crowd, but in the secret of their hearts they shrink
before its relentless justice.

The Bible acknowledges that the conscience can
be cluttered up with "dead works" (Heb. 9:14). It
recognizes too that conscience may be a constant accuser (Rom. 2:15). But since the blood of Christ can
purge the conscience, the Bible also offers cleansing
(Heb. 9:14).

In one of the great eastern universities, the president sent for a student and charged him with misconduct. The young man responded to the charge with, "But sir, there are not ten men in this great university who would not have done as I have done!"

"Has it ever occurred to you," replied the president, "that you could have been one of those ten?"

Very often we try to excuse conscience, but we are caught. This much is sure: when the Spirit of God begins to work within the heart and conscience writhes like a serpent, the cleansing blood of Christ alone can give it peace!

CHAPTER TWENTY–ONE

GRACE WITHOUT COST?

THE lady was mildly bitter about the situation, and this was it: For two whole years her upright, intelligent husband had been trying his desperate best to get into the Masons, and he had not yet succeeded.

That made me think. If this Nicodemus-type man had tried to get into the church, his two-*year* effort would have been cut to two *hours* or less! What a reflection on our modern interpretation of Christianity! In our despair because the crowd who wants to be holy is shrinking, we evangelicals have gone overboard in our efforts to get folk to join the church. In commercial language we have offered something like this: "Make your own down payment; then pay the rest when, where, and how you like."

Dietrich Bonhoeffer, in *The Cost of Discipleship*, puts it this way:

"Cheap grace means grace sold on the market like cheapjack's wares. The sacraments, the forgiveness of sin, and the consolations of religion are thrown away at cut prices. Grace is represented as the Church's inexhaustible treasury from which she showers blessings with generous hands, without asking questions or fixing limits! Grace without price! Grace without cost! The essence of grace, we suppose, is that the account has been paid in advance; and, because it has been paid, everything can be had for nothing."

No wonder this young saint, Dietrich Bonhoeffer, with head unbowed, went to the chopping block of Hitler's henchmen—and this less than a week before his prison camp was liberated. Thereby he proved his own philosophy: "When Christ calls a man, He bids him come and die." Dietrich himself was a martyr many times before he died.

To put it succinctly, the question plaguing me at the moment: "Are we offering too much for too little when we offer men salvation?" The way of the Cross was once a gory road; now it is offered as a glory road. Once the challenge was to take up the cross; now it is to ride a Cadillac and "rough" it smoothly. The offer to men is no longer the lordship of Christ in this life, but the promise of an all-expenses-paid, eternal honeymoon and a "mansion over the hilltop," with angel attendants and continual hi-fi music from an impeccable, million-voiced choir, world without end. How nice, but how unbiblical!

Hitler's philosophy seems to have been that if you say a thing loud enough often enough, folk are simple enough to think that they can have more than enough by what you offer. There is more than a slight smell of this in evangelism today. "The people want a painless Pentecost? Then let's accommodate them," seems to be the cry.

Having walked the "valley of the shadow of death" on at least two occasions, I think that for me death has lost some of its terror. But there are two things that I *am* afraid of: one, my lack of faith; the other, the judgment seat of Christ. I am not afraid that I shall get an unjust "deal" there ("Shall not the Judge of all the earth do right?"), but I am afraid that millions who have professed Christ's name will discover in that awful day that it is a serious business to bury talents.

The Apostle John speaks of not being ashamed at Christ's appearing (I John 2:28). That, at the least, implies that some *will* be ashamed. Again, John speaks of receiving "a *full* reward" (II John 8). That cannot but mean that some will have only a *part* reward for the opportunities which the years of their Christian pilgrimage offered. Though preachers think it too irreverent to state, they often clearly imply that this is the day of God's great "giveaway." They cry, "Salvation is a *free* gift"; and again, "He *gives* the Holy Spirit"—the implication being that there is no market, nothing to buy. There is no suggestion of self-denial, of discipline, or of Christ-imposed crosses to be borne.

The Book of God certainly makes it clear enough that we are going to be rewarded *for works*, both good and bad. "The fire shall try every man's work of what sort ⌈not of what size⌉ it is" (I Cor. 3:11–13). We *are* going to be rewarded for works. But—and this is start-

ling and stirring—we are going to be appointed *for*
what we are. Speaking to the church at Laodicea, Jesus
says, "I counsel thee to buy of me white raiment that
thou mayest be clothed." This white garment cannot
be the garment of salvation, for that is the gift of God.
The interpretation must be that what we *buy* is Christian character.

At thirty-five years of age, John Wesley lived on
about thirty English pounds a year, and fifty years later he was still living on the same austerity lines. He
will receive eternal dividends for it. Again, here is a
young doctor with a gold-paved road before him. He de-
nies this way, takes up his cross, suffers lack of funds,
and is criticized by unsaved loved ones. When the road
is rough, he fights off severe temptation to turn back
and seek the company of the comfortable, but "endures
to the end." He saves not only himself, but by his exam-
ple he saves others. I well remember an old, wrinkled
lady, red-eyed and hoarse of voice, who invested almost
all her time in intercessory prayer. Like Mary of
Bethany, she chose "the better part."

When the books are open (oh, those books—the
book of prayer, the book of tears, the book of criticism,
the book of fasting, the book of self-denial—these and
other books are but records), when the books are open,
I say, then all our human judgments will be reversed,
and the laws of the Kingdom will operate. The *last* word
is with God. Right now, we are all as spiritual as we
want to be; but then, we shall all wish that we had
been as spiritual as we think we are now. God grant

that we all live so that we shall not be ashamed before Him at His appearing.

CHAPTER TWENTY–TWO

"HOLINESS I LONG TO FEEL"

W HAT is our calling, our glorious hope, but inward holiness!" cried Charles Wesley. Then again he wrote,

> "God wills that I should holy be;
> That holiness *I long to feel*."

In this chapter we deal with the latter matter, that of feeling. Just here many would sternly warn us that our Christian life is not a matter of feeling. But though the old-time comment, "Ten million people can't be wrong," may be a good line for salesmen, it is a statement hard to prove when one faces the challenge of the millions who are lost or are following strange cults. Does bulk opinion really give immunity from error? We all cry No!

God is a Spirit. Man also is a spirit, living at the moment in the compass of fallible and corruptible flesh. I believe the poet is right when he says, "Spirit *to spirit* Thou dost speak." When the Spirit reproves,

how do we register it except by feelings? Have not
we ourselves *felt* we were in a horrible pit, and did
not a sense of vileness bring heaviness and a *feeling* of
lostness? Then, if we can *feel* lostness, can we not,
after the operation of repentance (which in turn
brings from God forgiveness), have a sense or *feeling*
of being lifted out of that pit, of having lost the burden of guilt? When our mourning (this we would certainly *feel*) is turned by our Lord into dancing,
would we not know a deep sense of *feeling* acceptable to Him because of this inward joy and the sweet-
ness of His pleasure?

The danger is to rely not on the feelings of the
heart but either on the feelings in the emotions or
else on the exuberance of a well-tuned physical body.
It is legitimate, says Peter, to have heaviness through
manifold temptations (I Pet. 1:6), for in matters of
oppression, impression, or depression, the believer does
not differ from his unregenerate counterpart in the
world. Such feelings are wearing, and can be exhaus-
tive and wearying. But exchanges in the spirit of man
are as natural as hunger and thirst to his body. For
instance, we speak of certain things giving a person
"a feeling of" security. The keen, conscientious student
might enter the examination room with "a sense of"
having mastered his studies; the traveler, with well-
stocked pockets, would "feel" adequate for the financial demands that the journey would involve. Both persons would have "a feeling of" confidence to stand
against oncoming tests.

So with the believer. Because Christ has "made peace through the blood of his cross" and each believer has entered by faith into that peace; because the Holy Spirit girds him in the inner man; because to the hungry soul, the Word of God is manna and meat to give strength for the journey—because of these wonderful and stimulating factors, the man of God can have a deep, settled peace in his soul, a peace which would in turn give him "a feeling of" security in a world of fluid circumstances. The Apostle Paul said, "None of these things *move* me." But he did not say, "None of these things hurt me"! I am sure he felt them but was grace-hardened against them. Likewise, King David cried, *"My heart is fixed."* Nothing else was—Saul plotted his death, Absalom betrayed him, his wife mocked him, death cast its shadow over him. But, with a fixed heart, David was more than conqueror.

Satan, with a permit from God, probed Job deeply. Strike one—Job has bankruptcy; strike two—Job has bereavement; strike three—Job has boils. After that, Lucifer is at the end of his tether, for he has no power to strike the soul. If this man Job breaks, it will be from the inside, not from the battering rams of hell. But Job triumphed. His is the most majestic utterance of faith in the whole Bible: "Though he slay me, yet will I trust him." This afflicted man might have felt his flesh tingle. Undoubtedly he felt an upheaval in his emotions. But I am equally sure Job "felt secure"— in a faith unshakable, a peace unbreakable, and a joy unspeakable when the gale of adversity, of calam-

ity, and of tragedy had blown itself out. The Spirit
had helped Job's infirmity and brought him glorious
stability. Even so for us Christians,

> "Let mountains from their seats be hurled
> Down to the deeps and buried there;
> Convulsions shake the solid earth;
> Our faith shall never yield to fear."

Or on the positive side,

> "His wisdom never faileth,
> His sight is never dim;
> He knows the way He taketh,
> And I will walk with Him."

CHAPTER TWENTY-THREE

LET'S STOP PLAYING CHURCH

WALTER Lippmann gives the Church a crisp slap in the face when he scathingly says that we believers are a group of "grimly spiritual persons devoted to the worship of sonorous generalities." Is that statement palatable, or does it set our teeth on edge? That is Lippmann's cultured way of saying that we Christians are sleepwalkers, not aware of what is happening around us, nor conscious of the direction in which we are going. If he is wrong, we can laugh off his jibe; if he is right, we need to do some stocktaking.

This much is sure: this generation is mesmerized by materialism and tantalized by T.V. It is jeopardized by evils no other age has known, and victimized by cruel, malicious propaganda that clouds reality and therefore confuses thinking. The last but not least ingredient of this "witches' brew" is the religious jackanapes, attracting the crowd to his revival jamboree with the lure of miracles, as a coverup for his itch for gold. What a day!

The enervated evangelism of the hour has left a trail of spiritual chaos. One of the top ten evangelists mourns that only half of one per cent of his converts endure. Another declares that a year after their decision, not ten per cent of converts show any sign of regeneration.

Out of their bondage, sorrow, and night, millions are crying for deliverance, for they are squeezed under the iron heel of communism. Yet free men heed their cries with little concern. Never has God looked down on more millions in human misery than at this hour. Before our eyes the unbelievable happens. International burglars, that is, the Communist section of the U.N., have convened in New York to masterplan the way to rob the rest of the world of its freedom. When did a brood of evil men like Tito, Castro, Gomulka, Novotny, and Khrushchev ever stalk openly into another nation's front room and, while planning its rape, partake of its hospitality? Here are men treading ground sanctified to the freedom of the nations, yet planning world enslavement. Here in a multi-million-dollar palace dedicated to unity, these political perverts plan world disruption and division. This is unprecedented in political records.

Political maneuvering and adroitness may stave off world enslavement, but unless there is a Holy Ghost revival, it will only push it back for a breathing space. Concerning the crucifixion of Cuba, there has been amongst Christians more anger than agony, and we have yet to hear of nights of concentrated intercession for Congo's deliverance from communistic castigation. Apart from Holy Ghost breakings, what will ring the emergency bell in the Church of the living God? When are we going to stop playing church?

Some see a star of promise in this sky of moral, political, and spiritual blackness. They declare with delight that before we can be enslaved by organized political evil, we shall at the last minute be raptured. Others are advocating the Christian gospel as a sure sign to prosperity. Why, then, were the saints in China who were subdued by Stalin not raptured? Why did God seem to stand by while South Korea was mutilated? Are we Western Christians a better breed and of better spiritual pedigree than they?

The enslaved might now be crying, "The harvest is passed; the summer is ended, and we are not saved." The people of Judah who in times past did cry thus, heard Hosea's call, "Ephraim is joined to his idols: let him alone." They saw the northern folk taken into captivity. But they sinned against light. God warned them, Jeremiah warned them, calamity to other people warned them; but on they went to their doom of captivity and lived to eat their own offspring. Eleven times in this book of Jeremiah (more times than in any other book in the Bible) we read, "God rose up early." God *tried* to intervene. As they made their first steps to calamity, He called them—but all was to no avail. At such a time, "Thus saith the Lord, Let not the *wise* man glory in his wisdom, neither let the *mighty* man glory in his might, let not the *rich* man glory in his riches" (Jer. 9:23). But when there is danger around we are prone to do all three things. Yet brains can *not* help us out of the jam we are in.

God has a controversy with the nations. First, I believe, He has a controversy with His Church. As with Israel, so with us. We have substituted organizing for agonizing, and equipment for "enduement." The world is not even mildly interested in our gyrating. Jeremiah's roots were deep. Read the first few verses of his prophecy. There God says of Jeremiah, "I formed thee . . . , I knew thee . . . , I sanctified thee . . . , I ordained thee . . . , I shall send thee . . . , I command thee . . . , I am with thee." Could Jeremiah ask for more?

My minister brethren, are we thus set about and buttressed with the exceeding great and precious promises of the Lord? The answer is a resounding yes—in this titanic end-time struggle we have the overweight of the finished work of Christ as well as the promise of Holy Ghost power for our commission.

I believe that at this hour the world is facing more solemn alternatives than she did on the eve of the Civil War. Few Americans doubt that this age needs a moral and spiritual revolution. Some time ago Billy Graham had the unique opportunity of addressing some 250 generals, admirals, and top-brass of the American forces. Fearlessly, Graham declared that he seriously doubted the moral strength of the nation if there should be a Communist war attack upon her. No nation is better than its church, and no church is better than its people. Only God-transformed personalities can change the moral fiber of the nation.

At the time of the Fall of Jerusalem, the voice of God, the voice of Jeremiah, the passing of three kings (two of them led into captivity), and the bondage of the northern people—all these stood in the path of the self-enslaving people of Judah. Today America, too, will have a tough time in committing spiritual suicide. What barriers are against her? There are so many that they seem informidable (but they are not). First, America must close her ears to more gospel broadcasts per day and per week than any other nation in the world. Next, she has to climb over a mountain of Bibles higher than the Great Divide. Then she must swim through a river of printers' ink, dedicated to the publication of tracts, books, and periodicals all calling her back to God. Certainly the endless belt of Bible conferences circling the nation is no easy grip to escape.

Another blockade against America's bid for bondage is the fact that she has more men under "alms" than any other nation in the world. The Americans are hilarious givers and dole out largely and liberally for missions and world evangelization. Shall this nation yet cry, "They made me the keeper of the vineyards; but mine own vineyard have I not kept"? Finally, America is blest with more Bible propaganda than any other nation and has more full-time and part-time preachers than half a dozen other nations put together.

This catalogue of divine favors makes stirring reading but is loaded with vast obligation, for America has the capacity to save herself *and* the world. The man with a loaded granary is obligated to feed the starving neighbors. We who have the awareness of the world peril and lateness of the hour are debtors to rescue what will otherwise be a lost cause and a perpetual blot on our spiritual history. Having the load of spiritual potential mentioned in this chapter, America can and must rise to write a new chapter in the history of the Church of Jesus Christ.

Emergency situations call for emergency measures. The sweet hour of prayer as a mid-week breather in the church has been reduced to a sweet twenty minutes of prayer. We sing awhile, have a Bible reading, review the immediate program of the church, and then wind up with a conscience-salving twenty minutes for stating needs to God. Would to God that we could raise a battalion of wet-eyed intercessors for this hour of unprecedented grief and spiritual peril! The slogan of the church must be, "We will give ourselves continually to prayer, and to the ministry of the word." *Every* church needs a prayer meeting *every* night of the week *right now*. Midday and all-day prayer meetings must be convened. God will welcome us putting Him to the test. How amazed He must still be that there are no intercessors! Denominational segregation must go; barriers must be eliminated and group prayer meetings formed. This is the crisis hour of the Church as well as the world. We must obey the Bible command to fast and pray, lest at the bar of God He say to us what He said to another, "Curse ye Meroz, said the angel of the Lord, Curse ye bitterly the inhabitants thereof; because they came not to the help of the Lord, to the help of the Lord against the mighty" (Judges 5:23). If we face up to the calamity of this hour, we shall get our faces down into the dust to cry, "Arm of the Lord, awake and put on strength." Out of these protracted prayer times would come a people glowing and growing, plus a whole new crop of last-day prophets. Let's make no mistake—they will come!

I was stirred to my depths the other day in reading of J. N. Darby (founder of the Plymouth Brethren). Before he became a belligerent theologian, he was an unctionized prophet. Born in England of Irish parents, he entered Trinity College, Dublin, as a fellow-commoner at fifteen years of age; and at a little more than eighteen years of age, he was a graduate with a classical gold medal. He entered the legal profession and was called to the Irish Chancery Bar. It seemed the road before him was paved with gold. Then God took over, for J. N. Darby was saved. Later he entered the Church of Ireland and was ordained a deacon by Archbishop Magee of Dublin. His was the life of a zealot. He roved over the bogs, moved in the Wicklow mountains, and was seldom home before midnight. Says one writer, "In an age of rampant materialism, the simplicity and frugality of his life rivaled that of the early saints. In middle life he trudged *on foot* through France and Switzerland. He subsisted at times on acorns, or welcomed a glass of milk and an egg for dinner as if it were a banquet." Newman says of Darby, "His bodily presence was indeed weak—a fallen cheek, a blood-shot eye, a crippled limb resting on a crutch, a seldom-shaved beard, a suit of shabby clothes and a generally neglected person." William Kelly adds, "Thoughtful for others, he was indifferent to comforts for himself. His clothes were plain, and he wore them to shabbiness."

This then is a stirring picture of the golden-brained man who was at that time the Apostle to the Irish Catholics. According to the record of Neatby, he won them to Christ at the rate of 600 to 800 per week, to the consternation of all. Darby's apostolic method and apostolic result came out of his meeting for nights of prayer and meditation on the Word. God is all Fire and all Power, and He longs to baptize His blood-bought Church with a baptism of fire and power— *that the world might know!*

CHAPTER TWENTY–FOUR

CASUALTIES OF OUR FAITHLESSNESS

THE answer to militant godlessness is militant godliness. In the lineup of "great powers," that is, in the power list, the Church has all too readily and without Biblical support conceded second place to the devil. This should not be. Satan and "principalities and powers" are mighty. Let none underestimate them. But the truth is that next to the power of the triune God comes the power of the Church (*not* the power of the devil and then after that the power of the Church). Next to the power of God comes the power of the Spirit-anointed Church.

The battle for the final showdown of power gets nearer. (Let no man be afraid. Many of us who read this chapter may yet wear a martyr's crown.) The underground forces of the devil have laid a magnificent strategy to sabotage the kingdoms of our God and of His Christ—the dynamite is laid; the fuses are set; the match is about to be struck. Apparently the honeymoon of the lazy Laodicean Church is almost over. Again I say, let no man fear—

for our sovereign Christ pledged the ultimate triumph
of the Church when He declared, "The gates of hell
shall *not* prevail against it" (Matt. 16:18). Never-
theless, this does not mean that hell's gates will not
make a mighty good attempt at the Church's dissolution.

The Bible alone gives a lamp to our feet for a
future. Without that lamp there is no illumination.
The days ahead will be grim. The Canadian Ambas-
sador to Egypt, who a while ago ended his brilliant
career by suicide, left a note which said, "All is
hopeless; I have nothing to live for." Bertrand Russell,
the British philosopher, says, "I wouldn't give a 50–50
chance that one person will be alive on this planet
forty years from now." The famed leader of the
FBI in America, J. Edgar Hoover, says, "The
twentieth century has witnessed the intrusion into
its body fabric of a highly malignant cancer—a cancer
which threatens to destroy Judaic-Christian civilization.
By this cancer one-fourth of the world's land surface
has been seared and blackened. One out of every three
human beings is caught in its tentacles. At this very
hour, some are wondering whether we (America) as
a free nation can survive the frontal and underground
assaults of this tumorous growth of communism. Just
one hundred years ago, communism was a mere scratch
on the surface of international affairs. In a dingy
London apartment, a garrulous, haughty, and intolerant atheist, Karl Marx, callous to the physical
sufferings and poverty of his family, was busy mix-
ing the ideological acids of this evil philosophy. Marx's
pernicious doctrines, originally of interest only to

skid row debaters and wandering minstrels of revolution, were given organizational powers by a beady-eyed Russian, V. I. Lenin, who, in 1917 with his Bolshevik henchmen, seized state power for communism. From that wintry day in St. Petersburg, communism began to flow in ever greater torrents." After Lenin came the crafty and cunning Joseph Stalin, and now the ebullient master-prevaricator, Nikita Khrushchev. Today, communism is literally a violent hurricane, rocking not only the chanceries of the world but seeking to capture the bodies, minds, and souls of men and women everywhere.

While the Church fails in nights of prayer, communism triumphs with nights of care, caring about the youth in her universities. *Time* magazine says that U. S. undergraduate capers would never do at Moscow University—where hard drink is as rare as soft homework, and posters warn girls that the way to hell is paved with Western cosmetics. Somber and sober, Moscow's students know that the road to the Soviet heaven is paved with education. Five applicants are waiting to take the place of every expelled student. For Moscow's science-impassioned students, the only alternative to honorable graduation lies in one of this year's extracurricular activities—applying for the distinction of being one of the first humans shot into space. This year there are 1,700 foreign students from fifty-three countries attending Moscow University. It has a total of 4,500 rooms, and its students are taught to take life seriously and apply themselves to

hard work. There then is the picture of political zeal-
ots bent on world domination.

The chief concern of many is not that communism
has enslaved a quarter of the world but that if it is
not stopped, it might enslave us! Recently I
read a statement from Mr. Khrushchev that the
Dutch will not hold New Guinea much longer. When
Russia has mopped up the lesser nations, she will be
able to apply economic sanctions that will force the
greater powers at least into agreement, if not submis-
sion. That is looking at the picture from the natural
level.

But there is another level from which we can view
the world situation, for after all, the destiny of the
nations is *not* in the hands of Mr. Khrushchev but
in the hands of the living God. Jesus himself declared
the indestructibility of His Church. Yet we can delay
its triumph. Some tell me that this preacher keeps
repeating the same warning. What of that? Is it
sufficient for a lighthouse to flash its warning of rocks
just one night a week? Ever-increasing danger calls
for ever-increasing warnings. If John the Baptist came
back today, he would not be a voice crying in the
wilderness but crying in the church. Political wisdom
has failed, failed conspicuously to arrest the progress
of Communist ambition and infiltration. Even in the
distribution of almost boundless wealth, America, the
most generous-hearted of modern nations, has failed
to check the triumph of Communist evil. The suffering

millions have fallen for the Commie's trap because, though given a new set of clothes and good food, they were still left in some form of slavery—either to vile conditions, hunger, or gross ignorance. A sample of man's inhumanity to man is in Congo, where crowds of skeleton-like children walk about vainly looking for food. These actually walk amidst diamonds, for two-thirds of the world's commercial diamonds are found there. *The Daily Mirror* of London, England, shows on its front page a weeping Congo mother with the corpse of her loved baby in her arms. It adds, "She has never heard of King Baudouin, nor of President Eisenhower, nor Mr. Khrushchev, nor Mr. Macmillan. She does not know why her country has become the battleground for ambitious politicians, a chessboard of cold-war rivalries between the great powers. All she knows is that her offspring call day and night for food that is not there, while planes bring in delicacies for the jaded appetites of folk in Leopoldville." Congo is a swamp of discontent where the mosquitoes of hate breed by the million.

Around the edge of Australia are super hotels, but in the middle of that great country there are stark-naked aborigines still living in 1961 B.C. These stare at jets that scream overhead with amused passengers, sloppy in foam-rubber seats, aching to touch down again in order to fill themselves at the troughs of Vanity Fair.

New Guinea stirs to the call of Mr. Khrushchev. For over one hundred years Christian churches have been there, mainly bordering the west coast, while the naked savages roam the trackless jungles in their frightful superstition and degradation. I marvel more than ever at the patience of the Lord with this Laodicean Church. Again I state the title of this chapter: The lost millions of this day are the casualties of the Church's faithlessness. God pity us! We bicker of post- and pre-tribulation theories, but I do not believe that at this moment these are vital. The devil will throw any red herring across our track so long as we do not wake to the damnation of this groaning creation.

Sleepers *can* be wakened! Zeal *can* do wonders! At the moment, the world is astonished at the economic revival of Germany. Crushed by two world wars but not subdued, she has risen—like a ghost—out of the wreckage of her cities and the strangling sanctions placed upon her by other nations. Under a disciplined economy and under the very shadow of Communist night, iron-handed politicians have not feared to call for tightened belts. But Germany bids fair to being a conqueror in world economics. Can not the same zeal, mixed with shame, grip the hearts of the Christians today?

A man who has traveled through much of Europe, the British Isles, Canada, and America writes me that he thinks America has passed the point of no return. I hope he is wrong. Repentance and contrition can work miracles. Never in my life as on this present world tour have I felt the criminality of the Church in withholding or neglecting to give the message of the

Saviour to men. The plight of the Congolese materially is terrible; but far worse is the over-all picture of world domination by the lust of the flesh, the pride of life, and the devil and his works.

The octopus of iniquity has this world in the tight embrace of its poisoning tentacles of communism and Romanism, as well as liberalism in the Church. Still more tightly it is held by materialism. I repeat (for repetition is the law of teaching), one thousand million lost people in this day are the casualties of the Church's faithlessness! If you are a spiritual juvenile—with your soul's mental climate wanting nothing more than immunity from eternal justice, escape from eternal fire, and a mansion on the main street of glory, with impeccable music from a hundred-million voice choir of angels—then this message is not for you. I speak to spiritual adults, to those who have become spiritual men and have put away childish things. To you I speak with a trumpet voice. This is our hour! *The next may be too late!* There is still a narrow neck of time in which we can have revival.

But (and this is the crux of the matter as I see it) we must *see* the plight of these lost millions. Statistics are not enough. As my old friend, John Sutherland Logan, says, "We cannot love a statistic." A world-famous preacher lifted his newspaper and read that a bomb had burned 80,000 people as crisp as bacon, *and he went on eating!* The statistics did not move him. Later, the horror of his stony heart burned him.

I have often been warned about being emotional. I fear cheap emotionalism. I also fear not to have emotion. (The man who has no emotion is an animal or a Hitler.) I fear the Christian who has no emotion—his soul needs a tombstone. When Luther saw a picture of the crucifixion, he cried, "My God, my God, for me! For me!" When Macaulay, the famed historian, saw the slaves of Sierra Leone, he was upset and could not sleep for days. William Booth, the revival trail blazer of 100 years ago, was so emotionally upset at the drunks in the London gutters that he could neither *eat nor sleep for a week*. These men *felt*, and then shook the world. Statistics can be stored in the deep freeze of the intellect and leave us unmoved. But let a man *feel* the plight of the lost, and he will do something about it. My blessed Master *saw* the need of the multitude and *was moved with compassion*. Is compassion possible without emotion? I fear not.

I am not a prophet nor the son of a prophet, but I dare state this without a blush or tremor: With a once-a-week prayer meeting, there will be no revival born in the Church. In the Acts of the Apostles, prayer was made *"without ceasing"*; prayer was made *daily*. Jonathan Goforth saw revival in Korea, etc., about 1907. He had been stirred to the possibility of it after hearing of the revival in the Kassia Hills of India a few years before. There on those hills for months they had daily prayer for the Spirit's outpouring, and *then* came the Holy Ghost deluge. So Goforth likewise got others to pray with him. Koreans prayed for months; nothing happened, so some withdrew discouraged. Goforth and others intensified their prayers; they prayed from four o'clock until supper each night. *Then* came the rending of the heavens. *Then* miracles were seen. *Then* whole areas were inundated with divine power. (Even animals were used of the Lord, as was Balaam's ass.) Let every church put a *daily* prayer meeting into operation this momentous year. Some will snub us as fanatics. Let them scorn. This much is sure: It is far easier to cool down a fanatic than to warm up a corpse.